YOU'VE
GOT
THIS!

Gill Books
Hume Avenue
Park West
Dublin 12
www.gillbooks.ie
Gill Books is an imprint of M.H. Gill and Co.

9780717190447

Edited by Jane Rogers
Proofread by Esther Ní Dhonnacha
Printed and bound in Italy by Printer Trento
Designed by Graham Thew
This book is typeset in 10.5pt on 16.5pt Calluna.

The paper used in this book comes from the wood pulp of managed forests. For every tree felled, at least one tree is planted, thereby renewing natural resources.

A CIP catalogue record for this book is available from the British Library.

5 4 3 2 1

YOU'VE GOT THIS!

Learn to love yourself
and truly shine in your
teens and beyond

TAMMY DARCY

GILL BOOKS

FOR SHONA.
YOU WERE RIGHT THERE
WITH ME ALL ALONG.
I WISH YOU KNEW.

X

WHO AM I?

MY NAME IS TAMMY and I have the best job in the world. Every day I get to meet amazing girls from all over Ireland who share their stories, and their hearts, with me and my Shona Project team. They inspire me and teach me and also give the best hugs (and who doesn't love hugs?).

The Shona Project was launched in 2016, but I suppose you could say it started many years before then – perhaps even back when I was a teenager. Our teenage years are very important in shaping the women we become. We start to learn more about who we are and to take steps towards our future. My own teenage years were tough. I struggled in school with bullying, my parents went through a messy split and my beloved sister became ill, which changed our relationship for ever. I felt very alone.

I created the Shona Project to make sure that every girl in Ireland has access to all the information, advice and support I needed back then. When girls support each other, amazing things can happen. When girls believe in themselves, we can change the world.

I hope this book helps you to start to see the amazing potential we see in all of you, and remind you that the parts of you that are different are your superpowers. Own them, cover them in glitter and shine brightly.

Don't be afraid to make this book your own. Highlight the bits you like, scribble your thoughts in the margins, turn down the corners, refer to it when you need a boost, and look back when you feel strong. And never forget to be kind to yourself.

WHO IS SHONA?

Anyone who has a sister knows what a special relationship it is; best friend, other half, partner in crime. Sisters share your whole life, and while one day you might fight to the death over the last doughnut, the next she will defend you with every fibre of her being from mean girls, or from parents demanding to know who ate the last doughnut.

My sister Shona and I are a year apart in age. We were incredibly close, but could not have been more different. Shona was calm, happy to lie in the grass and watch the clouds, always finding time to stop and pet animals or tickle babies. I, on the other hand, was a ball of energy, always trying to do ALL OF THE THINGS. I would turn every walk into a race, and every hobby into a competition, but she was never interested. It's very frustrating when the other person keeps letting you win.

When we were 14 and 15, Shona started to struggle with normal everyday things. Her balance and her memory were letting her down, and soon afterwards she was diagnosed with an acquired brain injury. We were told to prepare for the worst.

Surgery managed to save her, but left her with both mental and physical disabilities. Shona is still with us, but for the past 25 years she has required nursing care.

I lost the sister I thought I would share my life with. I thought we would share shopping days and chocolate brownies over lunch. (Who am I kidding? I would never share a brownie.) I thought we would go on weekends to the beach, or party together to remixes of the songs we had played over and over again on the ghetto blaster (look it up!) we got one Christmas. I thought she would be my bridesmaid, and I hers. I thought our kids would grow up together, and our own daughters would be best friends.

Shona was a beautiful girl, with so many dreams for her future, and so much potential.

We are all beautiful girls, with so many dreams for the future, and so much potential.

The Shona Project is a tribute not just to her, but to all of us.

WHAT DO WE DO AT THE SHONA PROJECT?

The Shona Project is a small army of amazing women and girls aged from 15 to 70 who work together to share our message of kindness, positivity and strength.

At the time of writing this, we have delivered workshops to over 13,000 girls in schools all over Ireland (and some in Africa and India), delivered huge conferences to packed-out arenas, appeared on TV and radio, and created an online community that reaches thousands every week.

We don't tell girls how they should feel or what they should think. We sit with them, we listen and we encourage them to think for themselves, challenge the messages they receive from society, and reassure them that every challenge is an opportunity to learn, and every day is an opportunity to start over.

We have won multiple awards, met with royalty, and told our story in front of huge crowds. We have laughed, cried, failed and triumphed together. We've had days where we don't know what we're doing, and days when we've been laser-focused. But every day we do our best, and that's enough.

Find out more about our work at www.shona.ie.

CONTENTS

SECTION 2: YOUR MIND

SECTION 3: YOUR BODY

SECTION 4: YOUR WORLD

WELCOME!

This book was created just for you. Through my work at the Shona Project, I meet amazing girls from all over Ireland every day, and the remarkable thing I keep noticing is that many of them don't know how truly amazing they are. A lot of the time I see that the things that are the most amazing about them – the things that make them unique – are often the things that they try to hide because they feel like they need to be the same as everyone else to fit in. I can understand that, because I felt the same. Now that I'm a little bit older, I've come to realise that once we embrace those things, we really start to love ourselves, to find our people and to really shine.

In this book, we look at what it means to be a girl in Ireland today – the good and the bad, the highs and the lows. My friends and I will share tips, tricks and life hacks and we'll get real about our own experiences and the lessons we have learned.

The book is divided into four sections:
Your Heart, Your Mind, Your Body, Your World

There is no one section that's more important than another. We need to take care of all parts of ourselves, all the time.

If you sometimes feel like you're not good enough, this book is a love letter from me to you. I hope you refer back to it when you need a reminder that you are enough, that you deserve to take up space in the world, which is a better place because you're in it.

YOUR HEART

IN THIS SECTION, WE WILL TALK
ABOUT ALL THE RELATIONSHIPS WE
HAVE WITH THE PEOPLE AROUND US:
FAMILY, FRIENDS AND ROMANTIC LOVE.
WE'LL LOOK AT HOW IMPORTANT THESE
RELATIONSHIPS ARE, AND HOW THEY
SHAPE OUR LIVES.

Your heart is your most treasured possession. Think about it. Your heart has always had your back: constantly beating, speeding up when you need more energy, and slowing down when you rest. When you're full of happiness, when you feel scared, even when you feel like your heart is broken, it keeps on beating.

Every. Single. Second.

But that's not all. Your heart is closely connected to and associated with your emotions – blissful happiness, aching sadness – and the love that you give to those who mean the world to you. It also acts as a safe for the love they have for you, storing it up to give you strength when you need it most. Isn't that amazing?

We can protect our precious hearts by only letting in those who really deserve it. Don't allow just anyone to come and break it. It's way too precious for that. Keep your inner circle small, with the friends and family who you know will always value your heart because they value you.

But sometimes you need to take a risk and give people a chance. Sometimes it pays off, and sometimes it doesn't. Unfortunately, getting hurt is a part of life. That's how you learn. But whatever you do, don't shut down your heart. Always be willing to let more people in. It's worth the risk, because it brings powerful life-lessons and friendships that will get you through the tough times.

Love is the most powerful thing in the world, and to love and be loved is the greatest gift.

RIDE OR DIES

'Show me your friends, and I'll show you your future'
MOOSA RAHAT

This is important. The people you choose to spend your life with will have a massive effect on the person you become in the future.

People who know your heart, push you to be better, care about your happiness, teach you and believe in you will bring out your best and give you the strength and confidence to be your whole self. People who don't understand you, pick on your flaws, encourage you to do things you know aren't right or make you feel bad about yourself will drag you down.

You decide where to set the bar. You set the standards for yourself. Decide what your values are and surround yourself with people who reflect those values.

WHAT MAKES A GOOD FRIEND?

We live in a world where people value the **QUANTITY** and not the **QUALITY** of people in their life. The social media world tells us that we need to rate ourselves and each other based on the number of followers or the number of likes we get.

This is wrong.

One good friend is worth 100 bad ones (or even 50 mediocre ones). Most of us can count our real friends on just one hand. These are our ride or dies, the ones we tell our deepest darkest secrets to, the ones we can see ourselves sharing our whole lives with. And these friends are rare.

Your friend group should feel like home, somewhere where you have belly laughs and ugly cries. There's no judgement and no one ever gets 'cancelled'. No one person dictates how everyone should think and act; everyone is just encouraged to be themselves.

WHAT DOES FRIENDSHIP MEAN TO YOU?

What is a real friend?

+ It's having someone who will always love you no matter what, but won't hesitate to tell you that you're out of order.

+ It's knowing that you can pick up the phone when you're at your lowest, and talk to someone who will just listen.

+ It's saving all those snaps where you can see right up her nostrils, because obviously they're going into a collage for her next birthday.

+ It's taking off your brand-new jacket because you know it will make her outfit perfect, and you can wear it another time.

+ It's a daily hug that renews your strength, because your best friend is like a human power-bank for your soul.

Friendship is a beautiful and unique thing, and you'll often find the best friends in the darkest moments.

Here are some friendship quotes to send to your bestie:

'Walking with a friend in the dark is better than walking alone in the light.' HELEN KELLER

'Lots of people want to ride with you in the limo, but what you want is someone who will ride the bus with you when the limo breaks down.' OPRAH WINFREY

'One friend with whom you have a lot in common is better than three with whom you struggle to find things to talk about.' MINDY KALING

'The best part about having true friends is that you can go months without seeing them and they'll still be there for you and act as if you'd never left!' ARIANA GRANDE

'My two best girlfriends are from secondary school. I don't have to explain anything to them. I don't have to apologise for anything. They know.' EMMA WATSON

'If we treated ourselves as well as we treated our best friend, can you imagine how much better off we'd be?' MEGHAN MARKLE

'Friendships between women, as any woman will tell you, are built of a thousand small kindnesses ... swapped back and forth and over again.' MICHELLE OBAMA

'The best way to mend a broken heart is time and girlfriends.' GWYNETH PALTROW

What does friendship mean to you? What kind of friends do you need? More important, what kind of friend do you want to be?

WHAT iS EMPATHY ANYWAY?

We hear the words 'empathy' and 'sympathy' a lot. They are both used all the time, and sometimes not correctly. So what's the difference?

Here's a simple explanation ...

Sympathy = I get ya, boo

Empathy = I feel ya, boo

Sympathy means that you can see that the other person is struggling, and you acknowledge it, but you don't really understand it. Empathy means you have a real understanding of what someone is going through, and you share in their pain.

We all want to be more empathetic. Unless you've shared the same experience as someone, it's hard to understand. If your friend is heartbroken, you don't get it if you've never spent a night ugly-crying while eating Ben & Jerry's. If your brother is slide-tackled in a county final and breaks his leg, you won't understand unless you invite that same brute to replicate his moves on you.

So how do you make sure that you are showing empathy?

Well, you LISTEN. How else can you understand? Ask them to tell you how they feel and try to relate it to a pain you've had that might be similar. (But don't make it about you, okay?)

Don't focus on the cause of the feelings; they almost don't matter. Focus on the feelings themselves – now, in this moment. If someone says they are sad, that's what is hurting, and that's why they need support. Sometimes people just feel sad, lonely, scared or anxious, so connect with that if you can.

What's the worst, most useless thing you can do?

Try to avoid saying sentences that start with 'AT LEAST'.

'I DIDN'T GET THE POINTS I WANTED IN THE LEAVING CERT.'
At least you can repeat and try again!

'HE DUMPED ME VIA TEXT.'
At least he didn't ghost you completely!

'MY MOM AND DAD ARE BREAKING UP.'
At least you have a mom and dad.

'I HAD AN ANXIETY ATTACK AT SCHOOL TODAY.'
That's nothing; my friend had three last week!

Pity and sympathy cause a disconnect between people, because you're basically watching someone suffer from a place of comfort. It's like throwing money at a homeless person while avoiding eye contact. Empathy allows people to connect on a deeper level, like sitting with that homeless person for five minutes and hearing their story, so you understand.

So the next time a friend is upset, grab the ice cream and dig in. Welcome to true friendship!

WHAT TYPE OF FRIENDS DO YOU NEED?

You really don't need many friends, just a couple will do. And they don't all have to be like you. Why not shake things up a bit and add some of these to your speed-dial list?

+ **THE RIDE OR DIE** – You know when you need a full-on, snot-down-your-face, mascara-streaked cry? When you really messed up, and you know it, and you need someone to not judge you, but just help you fix it? Or when you need someone to understand what you need without having to ask? That's your ride or die. They are rare finds, so hold on tight to these ones.

+ **THE ADVENTURE BUD** – The one who's always up for a new experience, whether it's meeting new people, going to new places, or trying a new activity. Want to try virtual reality, buy tickets for a festival, join a dodgeball club? She's your girl.

+ **THE TRUTH-TELLER** – When you're in that bad relationship, stuck in a spiral of break-ups and arguments, you need a dose of reality. Someone to tell you it's time to walk away, and remind you that you deserve better. Also, when you have poppy seeds in your teeth, someone needs to give you a heads-up.

+ **THE ZEN BUDDY** – When you're wound up, or angry, or panicked or scared, you need to be with someone who can help bring you back to earth. Their presence just calms you, because their energy is always super chill. Without saying a word, they make everything okay again.

+ **A MENTOR** – No matter who you are, you need someone who is a little further down the road than you and is willing to share their wisdom. Someone you look up to. Don't be afraid to make friends with someone a little older than you. They can give you advice, and you can teach them how to use TikTok!

There are also a few types of friend that you really don't need. A quick way to check if a friend is a good one is to ask yourself one question: do they make you feel good? If not, it's time to reassess how much time you spend with them …

+ **THE UNDERMINER** – This is a friend who, no matter what good thing happens, no matter how much you deserve it, or how hard you worked to achieve it, just can't be happy for you. There will always be a cruel little comment to bring you down to earth, a reminder of how, in her opinion, she's still better than you. (Note: She's not.)

+ **THE COPYCAT** – We often have similar tastes to our friends – it makes sense, right? But what about the friend who straight-up copies everything you do, buying the same outfit, repeating things you just said? You need to be kind to the copycat friend, because this is often a sign of low confidence or self-esteem.

+ **THE NARCISSIST** – Friendships should feel equal, but do you have a friend who seems to make everything about herself? She needs to be the centre of every conversation. She never asks how you're feeling or what's new with you. Generally, it's a sign that she doesn't really care.

+ **THE FLAKE** – You make plans, you book tickets, you arrange the trip. She's either late, or she cancels at the last minute; you can never rely on her. Before you judge this friend, make it your business to find out if it's because she doesn't respect or value you, or genuinely struggles with social anxiety. If she's struggling, go easy, and offer support if you can.

+ **THE NEGATIVE ONE** – Some people see the glass as half full, and some see it as half empty. And some think that the glass has a giant hole in the bottom and the water tastes like soap, always. Negative people can really drain your energy. Find people who see the silver lining in every cloud – it's contagious.

+ **THE GOSSIP** – This one usually starts their sentences with 'Don't tell anyone I told you this, because I'm sworn to secrecy, but...' The gossip seems to take pleasure in other people's troubles. Ask yourself: can she be trusted with your secrets?

Friendship is a two-way thing, so what kind of friend do **YOU** want to be?

I HAVE SOME IMPORTANT NEWS ... NOT EVERYONE IS GOING TO LIKE YOU

But that's okay! Honestly. And when you accept that and come to terms with it, it's quite liberating. You can't live your life like a chameleon, changing yourself to fit in with everyone – it's exhausting! Just pick a version of yourself that you're comfortable with and stick with that.

People are like flavours of ice cream. I might like salted caramel the best, but you might prefer strawberry, which I'm not a fan of. There's nothing wrong with either of those flavours – it's really just personal taste. There are loads of people in the world who like strawberry ice cream. It doesn't need to waste its time trying to convince me to like it or changing everything about itself to fit in with my gang. Sometimes I decide to eat mint chocolate chip ice-cream for a change. It doesn't mean that I've stopped liking salted caramel, but there's enough of it to go around.

Hopefully, at this stage, you've caught up with the ice cream analogy, and you know what I'm trying to say. People won't always 'get you', or appreciate and understand you. You will be so much happier if you make your peace with that.

Whatever you do, don't be vanilla. Sure, everyone likes vanilla, but vanilla is so boring. Be a mango-honeycomb-bubblegum-chocolate chip-peanut butter-coconut extravaganza. With extra sprinkles.

HOW TO FIND YOUR PEOPLE

Making new friends can be tough, especially in big schools where it seems like everyone already knows and gets on with everyone else. From the outside it looks like everyone else finds it easy, and that you are the only one struggling. Trust me when I say that this is not the case. All around you, people are just trying to fit in.

Try not to overthink how people feel about you, or worry about things you can't predict or control. Remember that we're all in this together.

Here are some essential hints for making new friends that a) are not cringey and awkward, and b) actually work ...

+ **DON'T PRE-JUDGE ANYONE** – If we were all alike, the world would be a very dull place. Give everyone a chance – they can't all be your new best friend, but it doesn't hurt to find some common ground with everyone you meet. If your best friend from primary school is in your class, and you spend all your breaks together, keep an eye out for someone who is alone, and invite them to join you. They will always remember your kindness.

+ **ASK QUESTIONS AND GIVE COMPLIMENTS** – Here's a universal truth: people love to talk about themselves. If you are struggling to think of a conversation starter, tell a girl that you love her watch/trainers/schoolbag and ask her where she bought them. Questions are great, because you invite the other person to say something about themselves. With a little luck, they'll ask you a question back.

+ **GET EXTRA EXTRA-CURRICULAR** – A huge part of succeeding in life comes down to just showing up. The same applies to friends. Just show up. There are loads of options out there for groups and teams, from sports to student unions to volunteering for causes you support to singing, dancing and banging drums. Challenge yourself to try at least one thing you've never done before. Finding a new passion is good for you, and you'll get to meet new people who are passionate too.

+ **BE CAREFUL OF BODY LANGUAGE** – Sometimes, when we're nervous, we close ourselves off from other people and can appear a little moody or uninterested. If you feel anxious or worried, you wear it on your face. Open your heart, relax, breathe and smile. I bet someone will smile back.

+ **REMEMBER: EVERYONE IS NERVOUS** – If you do find yourself alone, you might look around and think that everyone else knows each other and has someone to hang out with, but look closer. Everyone is open to making new friends. Be brave, and ask someone if you can sit with them. You will need to be brave for just one minute, but then it's done, and you're no longer alone.

+ **IT WON'T ALWAYS WORK, BUT THAT'S OKAY** – Sometimes people just don't get each other. It's not always personal, so don't make it personal. Don't try to make people like you, and don't turn on them if they don't. You're wasting the energy you could be putting into real and genuine friendships. Move along, sister.

Above all else, be yourself. You're fabulousness personified.

MAKING FRIENDS

I'd like to share the story of how I figured out the best way to make friends for life: by being the real me.

I always struggled with friendships in school. I don't know why, I just always assumed that people didn't like me. I come from a big family, and we were always encouraged to hang out with our many cousins as opposed to with other kids, so I wasn't used to mixing with new people.

When I started secondary school, all the other girls seemed so cool, and they had already formed their own friend groups over the years. Because they all lived in the city, they were allowed to meet up with each other outside school, often walking home together, while I was the culchie who got picked up at the school gate and spent all the rest of my time with family.

I was a bit of a nomad when it came to friends. I didn't have a group of ride or dies – I moved from group to group, getting on with people but not ever really feeling that I fitted in perfectly anywhere.

Halfway through second year, something happened that changed everything. One of my 'cousin friends' who was a year above me sat me down for a pep talk. 'I'm only saying this because I love you,' she said, 'but you really need to stop trying to be something you aren't. Why can't you just be yourself?'

I was really taken aback by this, and went quiet. I can't remember what happened next, but I know I didn't ask her to explain what she meant, or what I was 'doing wrong'. Instead, I went home and lay awake, wondering what about me was so bad that she felt the need to step in. What was it about me that wasn't real? I began to doubt all the friendships I had and I assumed that everyone else thought I was a fake and a fraud.

Maybe I was weird. Maybe I was hard to get to know. Maybe I was annoying. Maybe I was 'too much'. Clearly, I needed to change something about myself, but what?

For years, I worked so hard at being 'real'. I second-guessed everything I said, trying to be louder, funnier, quieter, more ladylike, cooler, thinner, smarter, less smart, more into make-up and fashion, less into make-up and fashion, more of a goth, more sporty, more edgy, more mainstream, more opinionated, less opinionated.

I tried on every disguise I could think of.

I became a fluid version of a person, changing who I was depending on who I was with, adapting to fit in, to become more like them. Eventually, the person I used to be was drowned in a million versions of someone else.

Now I know that to find your people, you need to be your own person. You need to be able to like yourself and be comfortable in your own company. You need to be able to accept that you won't fit in with everyone, and be okay with that. Those who do love you won't want you to change; they will love everything that makes you you.

PEER PRESSURE

'Do it now!' hisses your friend, 'Quick, while the manager isn't looking!'

Before you know it, you slip the make-up palette under your top and walk out the door, praying that nobody saw you.

'I can't believe you talked me into that,' you say, heart pounding and guilt-ridden.

'Everyone does it,' she says. 'Nobody forced you. Relax.'

You know you would never have stolen anything by yourself, you know it's wrong, and you already wish you hadn't done it.

You've just had a big ol' dose of **PEER PRESSURE**.

Your peers are people who are close to you in age, with similar experiences and interests. You have enormous influence over each others' choices and behaviours. For the most part, this is good. It's positive to grow up together, learning from each others' experiences.

When you were younger, your parents had almost complete influence over you, but as you grow up and become more independent, your peers play a more significant role in your life. You spend all day with them in school, and chat to them online when you get home. Our peers influence us because we want to fit in and find our place in the world.

We already know that the teen years can be tricky. You're trying to figure out your identity, your talents, your beliefs, and your place in the world. Your peers are facing the same challenges, which is a comfort to you as you make your way through life.

Peers actually have lots of positive influences on us – we can find positive friendships, inspiration and advice when we need it most. We can feel encouraged to try new things, get to know different people and build new relationships.

Then there's the less positive side of peer pressure, the side your parents warned you about. It's in our nature as teenagers to take risks, like shoplifting, drinking, taking drugs, or having sex before we feel ready. In the moment, we don't always think about the consequences.

Peer pressure can be subtle, or right there in your face: 'Oh come on, you big baby, everyone else is doing it!' You feel that to get approval and acceptance, you have to go along with the crowd.

There's always one person who starts, and then, slowly, all the others join in, making it harder and harder to stand your ground. This is when it's so important to have your values, rules for yourself about what you think is right and wrong. If you don't feel comfortable getting involved, trust your gut.

Giving in to the pressure to drink or try drugs removes your judgement more, making you more likely to take other risks. Know your limits. Always.

When you go to parties, be prepared for pressure situations, make decisions before you leave, and plan how you'll handle the conversation. If you start to feel uncomfortable, say you have a headache and call your parents to pick you up.

Eventually, you will get more comfortable saying no. And eventually, you will recognise the friends who are good for you, and those who aren't. The truth is that whatever choice you make in life, it's you who has to face the consequences. If you're not ready, stick to your guns, and ultimately, good friends will respect your decision.

WHY ARE WE SO MEAN SOMETIMES?

We all know bullying is an awful, hurtful, destructive thing, but it still exists in every classroom, in every school, all over the world. Why?

When people don't know how to channel their sadness or frustration in a positive way, it comes out in anger, and it can often be channelled towards one person who has done nothing to deserve it other than to be in the wrong place at the wrong time. For the bully, it's about feeling that they have power because, in so many aspects of their life, they feel powerless.

Remember this: Hurt People Hurt People.

Think about it. When you're having a bad day, feeling anxious or stressed or a little down, other people are so irritating, especially happy people. Bullies just want to bring everyone down. They think that for them to feel bigger, they need to make others feel smaller.

Here's the thing, though: while a bully might make you feel powerless, you can control your own reaction. Walking away without responding takes a lot of bravery, but try it. You'll probably find that when the bully doesn't get the reaction they are looking for, they move on very quickly.

It takes two to tango – it also takes two for a bully to be successful. It's a two-way interaction and both parties have some control over how it will go down. There's a great video on YouTube by Brooks Gibbs (look it up) in which he acts out a bullying scenario with a willing volunteer. Watch how quickly a bully will run out of steam when their intended targets fail to react.

If that doesn't work, speak up, tell someone you trust. Bullying is never okay.

If you're being bullied, here's what we want you to know …

+ **SPEAK UP** – You might be afraid to tell anyone, thinking that it will cause a big scene and make everything ten times worse. You might also be embarrassed about being bullied and not want others to know. Just pick one person you trust and start with them: a parent, aunt, uncle, teacher, coach, guidance counsellor or your doctor. If you've been holding the secret for a while, it will instantly make you feel better. Tell them the whole story, and they can help you figure out the right solution.

+ **DON'T BLAME YOURSELF** – You don't deserve to be bullied – nobody does – and it probably isn't based on anything you've said or done. Stop second-guessing yourself, wondering if there was anything you could have said or done or worn differently. It probably wouldn't have made a difference. Remember a time when you felt frustrated, angry, sad, insecure or powerless. When you don't know how to deal with those feelings in a positive way, you can feel anger or resentment towards those who seem happy. That's why bullies bully. They want to bring others down to their level. Never change anything about yourself in an attempt to please them.

+ **WE ALL WANT PEOPLE TO LIKE US** – Of course we do. But we live in a world where no two people are the same, and millions of different personalities have to coexist. Sometimes those personalities work well together, and sometimes they don't gel. We don't all need to be best friends, but we need to respect each other. Trying to be liked by everyone is exhausting. Let it go.

+ **YOU'RE NOT THE ONLY ONE** – There's an old war tactic called 'divide and conquer'. It involves making your enemies feel alone, so they don't all form an alliance and stand up to you. If you take a second and look around, you'll see that there are others who feel exactly like you do. These are your allies. Vive la révolution!

+ **WHEN THEY GO LOW, WE GO HIGH** – Take the high road, always. When you sink to the same level of behaviour, it only makes you feel worse, because you know better.

+ **DON'T LET THEM MAKE YOU FEEL INSECURE** – Bullies will make many different comments until they find one that gets the reaction they're looking for. They'll say you're too skinny, too fat, too short, too tall, too loud, too quiet. They'll pick a feature of your personality or your body, making it appear negative. If you buy in to what they say, those insecurities will stay with you for a long time. You're beautiful. Honestly.

+ **REMEMBER THAT THE BULLY IS NOT IN A GOOD PLACE** – If you could see into their world, you probably wouldn't exchange lives with them. They are trying to hold on to some form of control or power, to divert them from the things that make them so unhappy. This doesn't excuse any bad behaviour, but it might help you to realise that they are probably to be pitied.

+ IT WILL PASS – It's hard to see that now, but at some stage, they will move on. Bullies always do. And when that happens, don't be afraid to make new friends, try new things, or chase your goals. This experience has taken enough from you.

MY STORY: JEN

——

A RETIRED BULLY

——

Jen is now a grown woman with her own family, but she often reflects on a time in her life when she wishes that she had acted differently.

I hated school. I never felt like I fitted in. I never felt happy or confident; in fact, a lot of the time, I felt scared and worried. I convinced myself that if people thought I was tough, I'd be able to fool them all that I was full of confidence. People would pick on me sometimes, but I would always fight back and act like I didn't care. I did care, and I was always on edge, waiting for someone else to single me out.

AnnMarie was in my class from junior infants the whole way through school. Deep down, I always liked her, but if I'm honest, there was something about her annoyed me, although I couldn't say what. That annoyance eventually turned to anger. To this day, I can't explain it, although my gut tells me it was based on jealousy.

I don't specifically remember what I said or did to her, but I know it wasn't nice. I can't remember the words I used, but I remember how she used to look at me – a mixture of fear and confusion. I never thought twice about it, though. I just didn't care.

Now I'm an adult, and I work as a nurse who looks after sick children. Recently, I met someone at a party. She recognised my name and told me she was AnnMarie's cousin. Then she told me that AnnMarie said that I made her so miserable in school she wanted to die.

I will never forget how I felt in that moment. I wanted to throw up. How could I have made another person feel so awful and caused them so much pain? I was overcome with guilt; it hit me like a ton of bricks.

It frightens me, and I wonder why no one ever said anything to me about it. Nothing was ever spotted by the teachers; nobody ever contacted my parents. I wonder if AnnMarie ever told another person how she was feeling.

I read somewhere that teenagers don't yet have the brain development that enables them to fully understand the damage they can inflict on each other. As long as there are no consequences for these behaviours, they will continue.

We need zero tolerance when it comes to bullying. We need to make a stand. Schools need to talk more about how we treat each other. Parents need to make sure they teach their kids how to be kind, above all else.

The main thing I, as a reformed bully, want to tell you is that hurting others does not make you feel better about yourself; it will make you feel so much worse. We all know right from wrong, and we all carry the weight of our actions when they are harmful.

If you know in your heart that you have been mean or cruel to others in the past, draw a line under the things you did when you didn't know better and start fresh. It's never too late.

KINDNESS IS A SUPERPOWER

'Kindness is igniting a light in someone else for no other reason than to watch them and enjoy the glow.'
ANONYMOUS

Listen, we can all do better when it comes to kindness. We are all capable of taking our moods out on each other at times. It usually comes from our own insecurities. We've all done it. We've all made snide comments about how someone is dressed because they seem so confident. We've all talked about other people being so 'weird' when we just don't understand them. We've all hated on the popular girl because she seems to have it all, and all the boys like her. We've all excluded someone from our group because we feel threatened by her in some way.

Kindness is a **SUPERPOWER**, and you can use it all day every day, because it will never run out. You never know what someone is going through, and something as simple as a smile can change the course of someone's day. Scientists say that putting some of your energy into helping others, rather than thinking only of yourself, brings a feeling of wellbeing that lasts for a long time.

> **'People will forget what you said,**
> **People will forget what you did.**
> **But people will never forget**
> **how you made them feel.'**
> MAYA ANGELOU

Ask yourself this: how do you want to be remembered by those in your school? When you return for your reunion in ten or twenty years, how do you want people to feel when they see you? Wouldn't it be lovely if they remembered you as the girl who made them smile, who was there for them when they needed to talk, who was encouraging, positive?

How do you want to be remembered?

We can't all be popular.

We can't all be super academic.

We can't all be the best at sports.

We can't all be tall.

We can't all have silky smooth hair that doesn't go frizzy in the rain.

But we can all – every single one of us – **BE KIND.**

Most important, being kind should begin with yourself. Cut yourself some slack. Be gentle and be forgiving. You can start right now! Think about how you speak to yourself. Are you holding yourself to an impossible standard? Next time, try to talk to yourself the way you would talk to your best friend.

WHEN YOU KNOW BETTER, YOU DO BETTER

This is one period of my life that has had a huge effect on me, and is one of the reasons why I created the Shona Project. Having parents who are not together is quite common but can be stressful. This is my story about looking for happiness in the wrong place.

Until the year I turned 14, my life was pretty unremarkable. The only tension or arguments in the house were between the cat and the two dogs, but we mostly left them to sort it out among themselves. Life was boring, but good.

But that year, everything was turned upside down; we were hit by family break-ups, life-changing illness, and grief, blow after blow after blow. All of us were struggling, and the cat and dogs took to hiding outside or under the stairs. Everyone around me was falling apart.

I started hanging out with a girl in my class (let's call her Anna). She was going through the same thing as me at home, and we bonded over that. I thought she was cool because she clearly didn't care what anyone thought, and she had no time for authority.

Anna gave me my first cigarette, which made me feel so sick I threw up. Funnily enough, I continued to smoke afterwards. She also gave me my first drink, and yes, you guessed it, I threw up again, and continued to drink afterwards too. We skipped school to waste time lying in the fields behind our school, laughing at all the losers who were learning Irish verbs or underlining quotes in *To Kill A Mockingbird*. One night, she dared me to kiss a boy and said if I didn't do it, she would tell everyone I was 'frigid'. I did NOT like the boy, and the way he leered made me really uncomfortable. I kissed him anyway, to prove a point, which is a horrible reason to have your first kiss.

She seemed to love the fact that I would do pretty much anything she told me to. That was when I started to get into trouble, and that was when I noticed that none of my old friends were anywhere to be seen. They had given up on me. I was now one of the 'bad kids'.

My grades were slipping quickly, my teachers were getting more and more frustrated with me. I wondered where the old me had gone. It was time to turn things around. Without any big announcements, I started to spend less time with Anna, and put some distance between us. I missed my own friends, and started to spend more time with them.

Anna did not react well to the changes in our friendship. It started with some minor name-calling, the type of slagging that could be interpreted in a number of ways. And then the lines became less blurred, ranging from awful comments to straight-up threats. I would see my name on the back of toilet doors along with other names that became familiar over time; slag, bitch, whore, slut, even the C-word on occasion. Our house phone would ring at 2 a.m. night after night, waking us all up, only to be cut off when we picked up.

Any bit of confidence I had was gone. My entire sense of self-worth was based on one person's opinion of me. Which meant I was worthless. I couldn't eat because I felt so sick with stress and fear, I couldn't sleep or had awful nightmares. I cut myself off from everyone, and skipped school if at all possible. I became full of anger, just as Anna was, and started lashing out at anyone who dared to speak to me.

Eventually Anna moved on. I never really knew why – maybe she matured, maybe she got bored, maybe she found someone else to bully.

Looking back now, I realise that bullies take power by making you feel isolated and alone. It can be hard to see it at the time. They want their voice to be the loudest one you hear, and for their message to be the one that sticks. They convince you that you are worthless, and you believe them.

It's so important to remember that you're not powerless. You have the strength to overcome this, even if you don't feel it in the moment.

Take your power back. Look around you. Find the people who are also trying to be invisible, hiding away in fear. Speak to them. Never forget that you are good enough and deserving of happiness. The future is yours to decide. Don't ever let anyone take it away from you.

WHAT IS A NORMAL FAMILY ANYWAY?

Families are like snowflakes – no two look the same. A hundred years ago, Irish families looked pretty much identical from the outside, with a mammy, a daddy and lots of lovely freckled kids. A normal family meant having a lifelong marriage with biological children, with the assumption that the mother would raise the kids and keep the house and the dad would be the breadwinner and the boss.

People thought that 'normal' families were the best, but it turns out that many of these 'normal' families were not what they seemed when you looked a little closer. It was especially unusual to talk about mental health, and family members with mental or physical disabilities were sometimes sent away to homes where they were kept away from the outside world.

We were so full of shame and secrets that we were often deeply unhappy, and we were stuck in unhealthy situations because ... what would the neighbours say? Now we know that it really doesn't matter what your family looks like. The only thing that matters is that everyone knows that they are loved.

Some of us have one parent, some have two, some have four, and some have none, for all kinds of reasons. Sometimes relationships don't work out and people leave, or pass away, or live with new partners. Some of us are raised by step-parents or grandparents. Some have lots of half- or step-siblings. Anything goes, really!

Any group of people who co-exist in the one home, or across multiple homes, who care for one another and make decisions as a unit can call themselves a family. Sometimes you make a new family, one that makes you happy and loves you.

There is not one family on earth that's perfect, no matter how perfect they appear. Families are made of people, and people are imperfect, so when you tie together all those personalities, sometimes you get fireworks. Learning to understand and accept each other is a good start, but we'll never get it completely right.

WHAT DOES YOUR FAMILY LOOK LIKE?

We asked all the Shona Project Instagram followers to tell us about their families, and the replies were great! Here's a selection:

'My dad's dad left when my dad was young, and he had lots of partners over the years. When he was 70 he had a daughter at the same time as my dad had me. We're in the same class in school, and my aunt is one of my best friends!' – DOIREANN

'My mom died when I was young, and my dad remarried when I was four. I love my stepmom so much. I have never called her anything but "Mom", but we do talk about my real mom all the time.' – CARA

'When I was young, my dad left to live with another woman and her family. I struggled with it for a long time and went to therapy for a while for anxiety. Now I'm doing really well. I have great friends around me and live with my mum, next door to my grandparents.' – EMMA

'My parents had me when they were teenagers, but my mom realised in her twenties that she preferred relationships with women. It has always been normal for me.' – MELISSA

'My parents were never really "together". They've always been best friends, and both are now married to other people. I have siblings on both sides. Life is never boring!' – SADIE

'My dad is Nigerian, and my mum is from Nenagh! I love being part of two cultures, both of which always put family first. My Nigerian grandmother even taught my Irish grandmother lots of new recipes to cook for us.' – MEGAN

HOW TO DEAL WITH ARGUING PARENTS

Running a home and raising a family is tough, with bills to be paid, schedules to coordinate and work pressures to manage. Stress can build up, which sometimes leads to frustration and lashing out. If your parents don't always get on, the first thing you need to know is that this isn't your fault, and it's not your responsibility to fix it.

Living in a home that's full of tension isn't nice. If your parents argue a lot or if their arguments are extreme, I'm sorry that you have to go through that. But I promise you that you're not on your own.

So many of us who grow up in these environments think it's our job to make everything better: pressuring ourselves to shield our younger siblings, to act as a go-between or to defuse the tension by being funny or cute. This can have an effect on the adults we become and how we behave in our future relationships. We might be determined to 'not turn out like them', which stops us trusting other people or makes us run away from tricky conversations. It can also make us defensive or reactive, becoming easily 'triggered' by certain situations.

Remember that you are a new and unique person, separate from the people you grew up around. You will build your own life and experience your own unique challenges and triumphs. You and your future partner will learn to deal with challenges in your own way. Other people's relationships, including your parents', are not your problem to solve.

If your parents fight a lot, here is some advice to help you:

+ **FIND ONE PERSON TO TALK TO** – Everyone needs one adult they can trust and lean on when they get overwhelmed. That one listening ear can be your lifeline.

+ **DON'T GET INVOLVED** – Parents can try to drag us into their drama to back them up. Don't get sucked in. Tell them to sort it out between themselves.

+ **DON'T EAVESDROP** – You might hear something that you will later wish you hadn't. Stick on some headphones and let your favourite playlist drown it out.

+ **DON'T ASSUME THE WORST** – Arguments are a part of 99 per cent of relationships – they don't always mean that a couple will divorce. Sometimes arguments are healthy, and if they're dealt with maturely they can stop issues getting further out of control.

+ **IF YOU FEEL SAFE ENOUGH, TELL THEM THAT THEIR ARGUMENTS ARE UPSETTING FOR YOU** – They might rein it in a little.

+ **KEEP YOURSELF SAFE** – If you feel that anyone in the house is in danger, call someone. Disagreements are normal; violence or abuse is not.

Nobody is perfect, and that includes your parents. They are just people trying to figure out life and do their best. We are all learning every day, even the grownups.

If your home is not safe, and anyone is being harmed, call 999 or an adult you trust immediately. This information is about tension, arguments and rows – not violence or domestic abuse.

MY FAMILY BREAK-UP

Life is so lovely when you're young and think your parents are perfect. And then all of a sudden you realise they're not. Aoibheann shares the most valuable things she learned during a tough time in her life.

It was just before New Year, and we were all sitting around the kitchen in that post-Christmas period when you still wear PJs most of the day, and there are boxes of biscuits lying around the house. My younger sister asked why Dad had slept in the spare room. I hadn't even noticed, to be honest. I had just got a new phone and was spending a lot of time on Snapchat.

Mum called for Dad to come in from his office and 'tell us the truth'. And that's when Dad told us he was moving out. I was stunned. When was this decided? Why wasn't I consulted? I was the oldest child. I had rights!

Across the table, my little sister started to cry, and while Mum said very little, you could feel the anger emanating from her in invisible waves.

To tell the truth, I wasn't that bothered at first. I had so many things on my mind, like the boy I was obsessed with who had just messaged me, the fact that I wasn't sure if any of my 'friends' even liked me, where all those little spots on my hairline were coming from and whether I was expected to just keep having these periods for ever.

The next day, Dad moved out, and I soon realised that this was going to hurt more then I had initially expected. I watched Dad get into the car. As he stood crying in the driveway, Mum was crying in the kitchen, and my sister was crying in her bedroom.

It was only then that it hit me that things would never be the same again. Would we ever all be together as a family? Would I be forever torn between the two, trying to make everyone feel better? I missed my dad from the second he left, but I could never tell Mum just how much. I felt like I'd be betraying her if I did. I would hide in my wardrobe to ring Dad ten times a day as I couldn't stop thinking about him being alone in his awful, bare flat. I would shower Mum with hugs and tell her we'd be okay, and throw back the duvet every night when my sister, having woken from another nightmare, would come into my room.

I went from being indifferent to being really, really angry. Not just at my parents but at pretty much everyone, from my teachers to the bus driver. Being a teenager, I might have always been likely to go through this phase, but I know the separation just added to my insecurities and mistrust of people.

When I look back now, I see that my parents were doing their best to deal with real trauma. They were hurting each other, and they were hurting themselves. Now, when I think about it, I try my best to focus on the positives, because there are always positives – you just have to search for them. So here's what I learned:

First up, nobody is perfect, and our parents are no exception. We are so unforgiving of their imperfections, but there's something good about seeing them at their worst and loving them regardless. That love will see you through your whole life, because it's real.

Second, people fall out of love. The important thing is to learn from each relationship so that you can be better for the next one. Try to avoid repeating the same mistakes over and over. And try to leave the bitterness behind when you walk away.

Third, don't let your upbringing define you. Don't bring your hurt, fear and hang-ups into your own loves. Don't repeat their mistakes. Make your own ones!

WHAT iS LOVE?

Love is the answer. Always.

The word means different things to different people. But let's just ask the dictionary for the simple definition:

Love:
An intense feeling of deep affection
A great interest and pleasure in something.

It's a small word, but it covers so much, including affection, respect, warmth, protectiveness and lust. You can love your best friend, your grandparents, your pet cat and, above all, yourself. Then there's romantic love, the mushy, butterflies-in-your-belly kind. Google tells us that over 100 million songs have been written about love, but it can still feel super confusing.

The first time you fall in love is mind-blowing. Sometimes a stranger comes into your life, and sometimes you start to develop feelings for someone who's been right there under your nose for years. It can go from a 'huh, they're kinda cute' realisation to full-on obsession in no time. Your mouth goes dry when you see them, all the words in your brain just fall out, and you just don't know where to put yourself. Suddenly, it feels like those million love songs we mentioned were all written just for you, and for them. You doodle your name beside their surname surrounded by hearts and pick out names for your future kids.

And then what?

Sometimes people feel the same way as you do ...

And sometimes they don't.

And that really sucks.

Love rarely happens like it does in the movies or on TV. Love is HARD WORK! Unless you are a legit Disney princess who lives in a tower and has hair that's two miles long, you won't find love by lying around waiting for someone to rescue you. Rescue your darn self, girl!

It's really important that you don't expect a relationship to make you feel whole and complete and loved. You need to be all of those things on your own, and if you find someone who sees all the amazing things about you and encourages you to be more of that, then go for it.

The best relationships happen when two people who know who they are, and what they are worth, come together to share that life with each other. There is no instruction manual, you just need to figure it out as you go along. The important thing is to give your heart to someone who deserves it, and knows how precious it is, and then earn theirs in return. That, my friend, is real love.

HOW TO GET OVER HEARTBREAK

—

'If you are among the brokenhearted today, I am so sorry for what you are going through. I know what you are feeling. There's a hole in the centre of your chest that nobody can see, and it feels like your soul is leaking right through it. You either cannot sleep at all, or you sleep all day. You either cannot eat at all, or you cannot stop eating. You are either dead numb, or you cannot stop sobbing. You are either incapable of working, or terrified that somebody will make you stop working and then you will have to focus on your terrible sorrow ... I guarantee you – we have all been there. Every single one of us. And if we could survive it, you can, too.'

ELIZABETH GILBERT, 'A LETTER TO THE BROKENHEARTED'

So you finally told them you like them, and they said they really like you – as a friend. Or you've been going out for months and had made loads of plans for the summer, only to find out they've been texting your best mate.

Regardless of how it happens, rejection feels like someone has ripped your heart out and put it through a mincer. You've cried for days, had 50 emergency group-chats with your friends, and you've eaten ALL the Ben & Jerry's, but none of that works.

Scientists say that we feel rejection and physical pain in the same part of our brain. This is why, when you remember emotional pain, sometimes you actually wince as all the feelings come flooding back.

Rejection can also make you feel angry or blame yourself. You might think that you were rejected because you're not good enough. Logically, rejection isn't all bad. It doesn't mean that you're not beautiful and wonderful, but people look for and value different things in each other. You mightn't have done anything wrong; it's just down to chemistry and connection. The rejector might still genuinely think you're wonderful and worthy, but not in the way you hoped for.

How do you put yourself back together again?

1 **FIRST UP, IT'S GOING TO TAKE TIME – So give it time. You will get over it, and you will be fine, but maybe not today or tomorrow.**

2 **STAND YOUR GROUND – If there's a reason why it didn't work out, like maybe they didn't treat you very well, or maybe you**

weren't getting on, don't be tempted to get back with them just because of how it feels just now.

3 CUT THEM OFF – Unfollow. Delete. Block. You can't move on if you're obsessively checking their Instagram feed for clues.

4 DON'T HIDE – You can't stay under the bed for ever. Hold your head high.

5 TREAT YOURSELF – Sometimes, when you're in a relationship or crushing hard, you start to lose who you are a little. Get to know yourself again, bake yourself a cake, go dancing, buy yourself some new fluffy socks.

6 LEARN SOMETHING – Every challenge is an opportunity to learn something about yourself. What could you have done differently? Did you ignore your gut when it told you that something was wrong? Did you water down who you are to fit into the relationship?

7 REMEMBER THAT NO ONE IS PERFECT – Had you convinced yourself that they were? Take off the rose-tinted glasses. Nobody is without fault, and nobody is always right (including you – sorry!).

8 CRY AGAIN, IF YOU NEED TO – Feel those feelings for as long as you need to, and then get up and remind yourself that you're beautiful and that someone would be lucky to have you.

Finally, remember that you never truly forget anyone completely. Everyone who comes into your life is part of who you are and the person you will become. If they chose to leave your life, let them. Hold your head high and know that there are better days ahead.

When all is said and done, you don't need someone else's approval or love to feel you are good enough. You exist, and therefore you matter and deserve love, just as much as anyone else does.

ALONE VERSUS LONELY

We all want to be liked
... to be included
... to be popular

The world tells us that our worth depends on how many people surround us, both online and in real life. We need to be half of a couple to be whole. If we want to be seen as important, we must never be alone.

The truth is that while we need to connect to other people to thrive, we also need to be able to sit in stillness with our thoughts. This is the difference between being alone and being lonely. There are so many people who live their lives surrounded by others, yet they feel lonely. There are also lots of people who spend lots of time by themselves but never doubt that they are loved and valued.

Alone is a state of being; loneliness is a state of mind.

When you are alone your mind goes to places you might have been avoiding, replaying things you might have tried to drown out with noise and other distractions. But it also gives you space to sit with your feelings and become okay with them, to get to know yourself, to create dreams, to set goals and to just breathe.

Doing things *by* yourself can also mean doing things *for* yourself. It can be empowering, and you might even learn to love your own company.

Loneliness, on the other hand, can consume your thoughts even when you are in a crowd. It can stop you finding out who you really are. You will always find company in yourself. Loneliness can make you feel like you have to find that company in other people. Being alone is an art; embrace it. And breathe.

Here's a simple 'loving kindness' meditation that you could try. It creates both a love for yourself and a love for others, and it's a good one for when you're feeling a bit lonely. Find a quiet room and sit in a comfortable chair. Close your eyes and focus on your breath, but don't force it. Repeat these phrases to yourself, while thinking first about yourself, then about someone you like, then about someone you are neutral about and, finally, someone you find difficult to deal with. Give it a go!

May I/they be happy.

May I/they be healthy.

May I/they grow and develop.

May I/they be at peace.

WHAT DOES A HEALTHY RELATIONSHIP FEEL LIKE?

No romantic relationship is perfect, because people are imperfect to begin with. You may never be able to agree on what to watch next on Netflix or where to go for your anniversary dinner. You may struggle to communicate and have misunderstandings at times, but that's a skill you have to work on over time. You just need to figure each other out, and eventually you'll become more in tune.

So, silly, trivial things aside, here's what a healthy relationship feels like:

+ It makes you better, because they bring out the best in you.

+ You feel less afraid, because you know someone has your back.

+ You have chemistry, which can't be forced or faked. You'll know when it's the real deal!

+ You care about making it work, so when you hit a stumbling block, you talk it out.

+ It feels special, not another version of what didn't work in the past.

+ It's a partnership. You can't expect someone to come and save you; you both have to save each other, and build a relationship together.

+ You know exactly where you stand, because neither of you is playing games or mind-tricks.

+ You don't hold grudges or bring up past mistakes.

+ You treat each other with kindness.

+ A romantic relationship is not about finding your 'other half'. It's about being your whole self and finding someone who supports, admires and appreciates you achieving your own dreams while you support, admire and appreciate them right back.

WHEN LOVE ISN'T RIGHT

When love works, it's amazing. When you find your 'person', they should make you feel loved, important, and fulfilled.

It doesn't always work out that way, though. Most relationships feel great at the start, but over time some can get ugly. A relationship that makes you feel controlled, scared, uncomfortable or hurt is not good for you. If you feel like this, you may be in an abusive relationship.

Abuse can take many forms, not just physical. Emotional abuse involves manipulation, insults, control, blackmail or gaslighting. It involves reducing your confidence and self-esteem, sometimes slowly over time, so you stop trusting your instincts and don't have the strength to leave.

So how do you recognise a toxic relationship? Usually there are signs that we call **RED FLAGS**. These can include:

+ Calling you names

+ Telling you what to wear

+ Jealousy or possessiveness

+ Not wanting you to hang out with your own friends or family

+ Aggressive or controlling behaviour

+ Telling you that everything is your fault

+ Feeling like you have to walk on eggshells to keep the peace

+ Feeling unhappy more than you feel happy

Nobody wants to be in a toxic relationship, which is why we are sometimes so clouded by the idea of being in love that we forget what real love looks like. This is when we ignore the signs, mistaking these behaviours for loving behaviours.

Toxic relationships can sometimes bring out the worst in both people. Sometimes you need to take time to go back to basics and evaluate where you are. Are you happy? If not, face it now, don't make excuses. Be 100 per cent honest with yourself (which is a really hard thing to do).

Remember, anyone can find themselves in a toxic relationship. It usually gets worse over time, often so slowly you hardly notice it. It's vital that you feel comfortable talking to your partner about issues as they happen. If something happens that makes you unhappy or uncomfortable, you should be able to say to your partner that it's not okay. Put your own safety and happiness first. Set a standard for yourself when it comes to what you'll accept from a partner and never ever let that standard start to slip.

You deserve to be happy. If it feels wrong, it probably is.

WHAT IS GASLIGHTING?

Gaslighting is a type of abusive behaviour in which a person uses subtle and not-so-subtle mind-control techniques to make another person doubt their own reality and feel that they cannot trust their own instincts.

A gaslighter might manipulate the truth by telling you that an argument is your fault. They might convince you that you are paranoid or irrational or being over-sensitive, making you doubt yourself. They might try to convince you that your friends don't actually like you, or that no one else will ever love you like they do. They will convince you that your memory of or response to an incident was wrong, and theirs was right.

This behaviour happens over time, wearing you down bit by bit. Eventually, you start to doubt your own instincts, the very same instincts that are trying to protect you. Gaslighting can lead to low self-esteem and depression as the victim relies more and more on the gaslighter to form how they see themselves, their relationship and the world around them.

Always hold the truth in your heart. If you suspect you are in a relationship with a gaslighter, find somewhere safe to write down how you feel and read back over it, looking out for trends and warning signs. Talk to your family and friends, and trust them when they voice concerns, even when you don't trust yourself.

If you feel that you need to end a relationship with a gaslighter, it's best to end it completely and cut all ties. If you think there's a chance they might try to wear you down again, don't give them the opportunity. Talk to friends and family about what you have experienced and maybe ask them to help you reframe your perspective. Counselling might help too if you feel you need it.

If you ever feel you're in danger, or need help, contact Safe Ireland on 090 647 9078 or at www.safeireland.ie.

LET'S TALK ABOUT SEX!

It's time to talk about the S word. So let's do it!

In the olden days (as in the '90s and for ever before that), young people were expected to figure out sex and all it entails without ever talking about it. This meant that they had all sorts of assumptions and expectations that weren't particularly healthy. Those days are gone, and sex is no longer considered a deep dark secret that we should all be ashamed about.

Sex is nothing to be afraid of. In fact, when sexual relationships are done right, with open communication and loads of respect, they can be amazing, but it has to happen in your own time and only when you are both ready. For sex to be awesome, it needs to be safe, consensual and with someone you think is amazing and who thinks you're amazing too.

Whatever you do, please don't rush into anything, just to 'get it out of the way' or to keep up with your friends. Whether it's kissing or canoodling or going the whole way, here's what you need to think about before you say yes.

1 **ARE THEY THE RIGHT PARTNER? Do you trust them? You need to know that you can say 'stop' at any time, and that they will respect your wishes, and not hold them against you. You should never feel that you have to see it through or they'll be annoyed or angry at you. You don't owe anyone anything.**

2 **CAN YOU TALK ABOUT IT? The general rule of thumb is, if you're not comfortable talking about it, you're probably not ready to do it. You should be able to discuss what's about to happen, what is happening and what just happened.**

3 **ARE YOU SAFE? Contraception is not just to avoid pregnancy, it's also vital in order to prevent sexually transmitted diseases. This may involve a combination of different types of contraception such as condoms, the pill, IUDs, etc. Having a sexual relationship comes with a responsibility to educate yourself on safety. Go talk to your GP or find out more on www.mycontraception.ie.**

4 **AT THE END OF THE DAY, NO ONE CAN TELL YOU WHEN YOU'RE READY** – It's entirely up to you and you alone. Be safe, be informed and be comfortable.

Finally, don't think that you will learn much about real sex from porn, because it's not very realistic. See page 133 for more on this.

The legal age for sexual activity in Ireland is 17, regardless of gender or sexual orientation. It's important that you know this!

CONSENT EXPLAINED

Let's go back to that word **CONSENSUAL** for a sec. What does that mean?

When, how and with whom you have sex is up to you and you alone. You need to do it at your own pace and on your own terms. No matter what you've seen on TV or what you hear from your friends, you have to be ready. Sex isn't just physical, it's emotional too, so it's key that you're comfortable about it.

We can overcomplicate conversations around consent, but really it just comes down to making sure that every sexual experience you have is based on mutual respect.

When you respect someone, you care about their feelings, you try to understand their needs and you make sure that you don't cross their boundaries or make them uncomfortable. It's very simple.

You wouldn't help yourself to someone's food or take something from their bag without asking first if they're okay with it. If they weren't comfortable with it, you would accept their wishes.

And that, my friends, is CONSENT 101.

Asking someone if they're okay and checking in with them is in no way a turn-off. Both people feeling seen and appreciated will actually add an extra level of trust, connection and communication to the experience.

There is loads of pressure on you as a teenager to keep up with what you imagine everyone else to be doing. But please take your time. All your sexual experiences, and especially your first, should be at your own pace and with a person you feel comfortable with. Your relationship with sex is yours and yours alone. Don't worry if the rest of the world appears to be having a great time, it's all smoke and mirrors really. You'll often hear from others how 'amazing' their sex lives are, but they might have the same concerns and worries that you have.

Just like when buying knickers in Penneys, comfort is key. Try not to agree to doing anything you're not comfortable with just because you don't want to make them uncomfortable. If they're the right person, they wouldn't want that – and your comfort should be key for them too.

Trust is also really important. Ideally, when you look back on your first time, you will remember it as a positive experience, one that you were ready for and one that was pleasurable for you – apart from those first-time nerves.

Consent is:

+ **POSITIVE** – A clear and spoken 'Yes', not just the absence of a no.

+ **ACTIVE** – Silence is not consent; participation is not consent.

+ **FREELY GIVEN** – 'No' does not mean 'Ask me until it turns into a "yes"'. Consent isn't something you can be pressured into. You also have the right to change your mind at any time. Consent cannot be given if you are incapacitated by drugs or alcohol.

+ **ONGOING** – Just because you agree to one behaviour doesn't mean you agree to another; just because you agree at one time does not mean you agree at another time.

Consent is ALL of these things, and it is also **ENTHUSIASTIC!**

THE MANY SHADES OF SEXUALITY

We're generally not into labels because everyone is different and unique. We shouldn't need to find a box that we fit neatly inside so that everyone knows and understands us. As a society we're changing rapidly, trying to find new ways to respect and protect each other. And that's a good thing.

When it comes to sexuality and gender identity, there are lots of different terms and definitions, which can change all the time.

The key is to allow people to tell you in their own time how they identify and to respect that. No judgement should ever be placed on a person's label, and they shouldn't ever be compared in terms of their value. People are people and love is love, and to be honest, it's really nobody else's business.

Whether you are a member of the LGBT+ community, or whether you want to be an ally to that community, here is a helpful list of terms and their explanations:

+ **ALLY** – A cis and straight friend of the LGBT+ community who believes in the social and legal equality of all people.

+ **ASEXUAL** – A person who isn't interested in sexual relationships or does not feel sexual attraction. Also known as Aces.

+ **BISEXUAL** – A person who is attracted to more than one gender.

+ **CISGENDER** – A person who is not trans, having been assigned the correct gender at birth. In other words, someone who is assigned male at birth and also identifies as a man, or someone who is assigned female at birth and identifies as a woman.

+ **DEMISEXUAL** - A person who feels sexual attraction only to people with whom they have an emotional bond.

+ **GAY** – This word is often used to describe all same-sex attraction but it usually refers to men who are attracted to men.

+ **GENDER IDENTITY** – Your own sense of being a male, female or non-binary.

+ **HETEROSEXUAL/STRAIGHT** – A person who is not attracted to people of their own gender.

+ **INTERSEX** – A person who is born with ambiguous sexual organs that don't completely match those of either a man or woman.

+ **LESBIAN** – A woman who is attracted to other women.

+ **LGBT, LGBT+ LGBT*, LGBTQAI+** – These are terms for lesbian, gay, bisexual, transgender and related communities (queer, intersex and asexual). People use different acronyms depending on their perspective. This book generally uses 'LGBT+', although some contributors prefer a different term. Choose whichever term works for you.

+ **NON-BINARY** – An umbrella term for gender identities that fall outside male and female.

+ **PANSEXUAL** – A person who is attracted to another person regardless of gender or sexual preference.

+ **PRONOUNS** – The words we use to describe people's identity: she/her, he/him or they/them. If you're not sure, use their first name or they/them until you figure it out.

+ **QUEER** – A broad term that is often used as an umbrella term for the LGBT+ community and can refer to sexuality or gender identity. This word can be used as a negative slur but has recently been reclaimed to represent all things queer.

+ **QUESTIONING** – A person who is still figuring out who they are. Nobody should ever be rushed when it comes to how they identify.

+ SEXUALITY – Who you are attracted to.

+ TRANSGENDER/TRANS – This word is used for all sorts of people whose identity, or general sense of self, does not conform with what is typically associated with the sexual organs they were born with. Some trans people take medical steps to align their bodies with their genders, and some don't. It is not okay to ask anybody personal questions about their bodies.

The LGBT+ community is beautiful, vibrant and inclusive, and it is celebrated each year during Pride. Pride is represented by the rainbow flag, and a parade celebrating it is held in most large cities and towns in Ireland and across the world.

The most important thing is to treat everyone with the love and respect they deserve, and remember that everyone should feel safe and supported in being their whole selves.

If you have more questions, ShoutOut.ie is a great organisation providing support and advice to the LGBT+ community.

ADVICE ON COMING OUT

Alana was one of the first Shona ambassadors. I first met her in 2016, just before she completed her Leaving Cert. Over the years we have had many a chat, and she never fails to teach me something.

Dear Little Questioning Beauty,

There is no doubt that the next few years of your life will see you do some amazing things. But you're going to face your struggles too. One being falling in and out of love not only with someone else but with yourself. Your sexuality can be something scary, especially in the beginning, and I promise someday it will be a great source of happiness for you. Here are a few of the tips I wish I had gotten when I was hidden under the dresses and cashmere jumpers in my closet way back when.

Relax. Breathe. You haven't changed.

So maybe you're freaking out about this new discovery, worried about what your friends and family will think of you as this new 'changed' person. Let me break this to you gently: you are still you, as much you as you were before you thought you might be queer. You've learned about a part of yourself you didn't know existed. That's not a change

– that's an adventure, a chance for you to find out about yourself and meet some wonderful people in the process. Take a deep, glitter-filled breath in through your nose and know that this is you, and you should be so proud of knowing yourself well enough to identify it.

Come out for yourself

Coming out is something you'll do throughout your life. It gets easier, but that doesn't mean that you won't have days when you just don't want to talk about it – and that's okay. Make sure coming out is something you want, not something that is expected of you. Come out in your own time to the people you want to come out to. Don't rush it. If people aren't okay with your sexuality, be open to the reasons why they feel this way, but also understand that your sexuality is not your fault and you can't change that part of yourself. Please remember that you aren't selfish for coming out; you are wonderful, brave and an absolute queen for wanting to be honest with your feelings.

You know yourself better than anyone else

Some people will ask questions (even if it's none of their business) and while that's normal, that doesn't mean you have to put up with it. People might ask, 'How do you know you're gay/lesbian/bisexual/pan/demi?' or 'Are you sure?' While these questions are valid, you know what your heart wants at the end of the day, so don't feel like you have to answer if you don't want to.

Find out about the community

Meeting other LGBT* young people can be a struggle and also kind of scary, especially if you're in a rural area or a small town, but that doesn't mean they aren't there. See if there is an LGBT* youth group in your area, or if there is a college nearby, drop them an email if you *have questions. And, of course, have a look online for information. BeLonGTo.org, SpunOut.ie and B4UDecide.ie all have resources for people coming out or who might be questioning. As a general rule of thumb, no research is bad research.*

Don't feel bad for falling in love

I get it. Girls are awesome – even straight girls can totally admit that. It's tough when you are a queer teen. Often when you meet another person who also operates in LGBT* circles, it can be difficult to tell the difference between an intense friendship and a crush. All the butterfly-in-your-stomach feelings are heightened because, unlike other girls your age, you usually never have the chance to find other girls like you. So, it's completely acceptable to fall head over heels for the first wonderful girl with pretty brown eyes and an affinity for plaid. However, it can (and will) hurt when feelings aren't reciprocated and that just sucks. Whether you fall for someone who is also attracted to the same sex, or for a girl who is straight, you can't change their heart to beat with yours, just like people can't convince you to be straight.

Definitions are for dictionaries

There is a huge pressure when coming out to define yourself as something – whether that be gay, lesbian, bisexual, pansexual or whatever floats your lady-boat. Please remember there isn't something wrong if you don't feel an instant connection with a label or if you never feel a connection. Another thing I heard when I was coming out that really helped me was 'Don't be a prisoner of a label.' You could be bisexual one day, gay the next and asexual the day after. This is your life. We don't belong to people, nor should we have to accept an identity if we are seeing someone. You are more than a label. You are an entire person separate from your sexuality.

There is no right or wrong way to come out. It's different for everyone because everyone has different circumstances and supports, and you need to consider yours. Just do it your way, be authentic and true to yourself and you can't go far wrong. I'm still learning. I learn something every single day. Some days are more difficult than others, but I live for the good days.

Chase your rainbows and enjoy the trip!

INTERVIEW: ALEX

———

MY TRANSITION STORY

———

A large part of the LGBT+ community, but one that is often silenced, is the ever-growing transgender (or trans) community. Trans people often face more oppression than other members of the community, with threats of sexual assault and physical violence looming over their very existence. The often unaccepting social atmosphere severely impacts the mental health of trans people, with many self-harming and attempting suicide in order to escape the social pressures of performing a gender they don't feel represents them. Here, Alexandra Day speaks about her experience coming out as trans.

When and how did you know you were trans?
I knew that I didn't want to be a boy from about 8 or 9, but I didn't actually have the language to describe what I was feeling until I

randomly stumbled across an article about trans people when I was 15. It was this eureka moment because the more I looked into it, the more I found the words I needed to describe the disconnect between my gender identity and the person I presented to the world every day.

How did you feel about being trans?

I was apprehensive at first because I knew it would send me on a different path in life to the one I was on. However, as more time passed, I realised that a life where I never came out and truly accepted myself would mean going through life as a ghost. I would always struggle with people getting close to me because of this secret I had.

What/who helped you come to terms with being trans?

I was in third year of college and felt that I'd reached a crossroads in life. One path was living my old life and trying to make the best of things. The other was coming out and accepting myself for who I truly was, and although it would be the tougher path, it would ultimately be more rewarding. I felt like I would be wasting my life if I had chosen the first path.

Tell us your coming-out story.

I came out to my younger sibling first. Even before I had told them they were always fiercely supportive of social justice issues in general, and particularly LGBTQIA+ issues. I knew that they would be incredibly supportive so I felt comfortable coming out to them. We stayed up chatting for about three hours after I told them, just discussing how long I'd known, when I decided to come out, and so on.

For more information or guidance please check out TENI, who do great work in this area (www.teni.ie).

UNDERSTANDING ASEXUALITY

Amber is another Shona ambassador, and one of the smartest people I've ever met. I love this piece, in which she beautifully describes asexuality in a way that really helped me to understand it.

I want to talk about a sexuality that's largely forgotten about and glossed over – hell, it's not even in LGBT. (Sometimes, it's written as LGBTQIA+.)

And in answer to the commonly asked question, no, I don't reproduce like a plant. God, I wish.

So what exactly is asexuality?

Asexuals don't experience sexual attraction. This doesn't mean we can't/won't have sex, since it is physical stimulation of the body, but personally I have no desire to sleep with anyone.

The consensus of 'sexual attractiveness' flies right over my head. Of course, I know the conventional standards – nice features, symmetrical face – but it takes me at least a minute of talking to someone whom the majority of people would describe as 'hot' to realise it. And when I do, there's no reaction.

I don't know how to explain what's missing because I don't know what sexual attraction feels like. It's as if the link between noticing someone's hot or attractive or my type and being actually attracted enough to them to want sex with them is gone.

'But', you may be thinking, 'everyone has their own type of person they're attracted to. Everyone's different in their preferences. We all don't agree on what makes a person sexy.'

Maybe I just haven't seen what I prefer yet in my nineteen short years of life?

Asexuality is different from being extremely picky about who we are attracted to. It's the complete absence of wanting a physical relationship with someone because their body is attractive.

When did I first hear about asexuality?

I don't remember when I first read about asexuality, but I remember being drawn to it, as if it fitted. The more I read about it and the different sub-sections and definitions, the more it fitted me. I was lucky enough to know someone who identified as asexual who could answer all my questions about it, and I am forever grateful to them. I have only encountered one confirmed asexual character in the media, and that is Raphael from [the programme] Shadowhunters. In general, any character who could possibly be coded as asexual at the start of a show or film usually finds that 'special someone' who makes them believe in love and sex again – it's as if everyone on earth needs to be paired off and reproduce.

In my experience, realising you're asexual is different from realising you're gay – you don't have conflicting feelings to wrestle with, or have to fight against what you've been taught is right or bullied for it – it's just the vast, vague sense that the world all around you knows something you don't. Like it operates on a desire absent in you. It's not traumatising, just ... confusing. The emphasis on sex in advertisements, in films, books, TV series is so massive, and yet I still don't understand it.

If you are questioning or feel like unknown things seen by all fly right by you, maybe you're asexual.

Or maybe you don't feel that way, but know more about asexuality now, and that's enough.

WHO ARE YOUR PEOPLE?

The person you become is moulded, sculpted, formed and painted by the people in your life. This includes the good and the not so good: those who teach you, encourage you, support you, love you, hurt you, leave you, neglect you and inspire you.

It starts with your family – your siblings, parents – and expands outwards like a giant web to include your great-aunt Brigid and the third cousin you have never met. Add in the neighbours, your teachers and coaches, the guy or girl you've been texting, your frenemies and the school caretaker.

Now let's add another layer to include all the people who you might not ever meet in person, but who exist in your online world, popular MUAs, your favourite brands, stars of *Love Island* (and their fashion collabs), Michelle Obama, Rupi Kaur, Brené Brown and the people you aspire to be like.

Think of yourself as part of a big chain consisting of the generations who came before you, and those who will come afterwards. While it might sometimes feel like the older generation don't get you, don't underestimate how much good advice they can give you. Sure, maybe they don't know what TikTok is (TokTok? Ticktick? Tickitytocks?), but they have all experienced heartbreak, struggled with knowing who they are and learned more about how people work than you can imagine.

If you were to draw that family web, who would be in it? Think of how much goodness, strength and wisdom is floating around you all the time. Use it!

If you have grandparents in your life, why not get to know them better by asking them questions about when they were growing up? They probably have loads of interesting or funny stories to share.

DEALING WITH ENDINGS

Goodbyes are tricky, and we're really not that good at dealing with them. What does your ma say when she's ending a phone call with her sister? Byebyebyebyebyebyebyebyebyebye ...

Endings come in all shapes and sizes: realising that your sister ate the last of the Rice Krispies; friendships that don't work out; things we hoped for that didn't happen for us (this time); moving on to new phases of our life; family break-ups; and, hardest of all, when a loved one passes away.

When someone you know dies, grief hits hard, and there are lots of emotions tied up in the whole experience: sadness, anger, despair, confusion, disbelief. It's important to remember that everyone reacts differently, and all our experiences are unique to us.

Here's what we want you to know if you ever experience grief: it hurts. Really, really hurts. But the pain you experience is a testament to the love you shared with the person who has passed away. If the scar runs deep it means the love ran deep too. And you will never, ever regret that part.

There is no formula for grief. It is a process that will pass at its own pace. It comes in waves, and some days all you can do is float and wait for things to calm down. Other days, you will need to cling to something or somebody because you are tired and you can't do it by yourself. One day, you'll find that you can touch the bottom of the water with your toes, and eventually your two feet will support you completely.

The waves will never completely disappear, but that's okay, you will become an expert swimmer. You will get through it. I promise.

SECTION 2

YOUR MIND

DID YOU KNOW THAT YOUR BRAIN
PROCESSES SOMEWHERE BETWEEN
60,000 AND 80,000 THOUGHTS PER DAY?
THAT'S AN AVERAGE OF 2,500 TO 3,300
THOUGHTS PER HOUR! WOW!

These thoughts are made up of a mixture of the positive (learning, problem-solving, snapshots of beautiful sights and amazing memories, reminders for you to stay hydrated and get enough sleep) and the negative (telling yourself that you're not good enough, worrying, stressing and those down days).

In this section, we'll chat about ways in which you can help your brain and your mind to be at their best.

YOUR MINDSET

Your mindset is basically your outlook on life, your approach to challenges and your overall attitude.

Having a **POSITIVE** mindset is something you can learn, and there are many ways to do this. A crucial part of this is thinking about how you talk to yourself. **NEGATIVE** self-talk really harms how you view yourself and the world around you. Sometimes things are just sad or bad, and it's okay to feel down or stressed from time to time. In general, though, positivity is a habit. This section is all about how to train your mind to see the best in life.

Here are some mindset hacks and tricks:

+ START A GRATITUDE JOURNAL – Every day, list three things you're grateful for, like the garlic bread you had with your pizza for dinner, the fluffy socks that kept your toes warm, the fact that your parents drove you to school so you didn't have to walk in the rain. The trick is never to list the same things twice. This means you have to actually seek out good things every day, which means your mind is focused on positivity.

+ FIND THE GOOD IN THE BAD – When you make a mistake, or when your heart is hurting, don't feel hopeless. Look for the opportunity, or the learning. It's always in there somewhere. It makes the light at the end of the tunnel that little bit brighter.

+ SURROUND YOURSELF WITH POSITIVE PEOPLE – Those who see the good in life are the most fun to be around. Your interactions with them will energise you and remind you of all the amazing things in the world.

SIX THINGS YOU NEED TO STOP DOING, BECAUSE THEY'RE NOT GOOD FOR YOU

There are lots of things that are bad for us, such as smoking, staying up too late, or wearing a bra that's too tight. But there are other bad habits that we should avoid in order to live a happy and healthy life. How many of these do you need to quit? Let's all go cold turkey together.

1 BITCHING AND GOSSIPING – If you feel the urge to say something mean about someone else, stop right there. That urge usually comes from somewhere deep inside and is a sign that something is going on with us. There is never a good reason to put hate or negativity out into the world. Be kind.

2 **WORRYING ABOUT THINGS YOU CAN'T CONTROL** – The number of things you can worry about is infinite, but the number of those things you can control is minuscule. Remember – you can't control what people think of you or how they behave. You can only be responsible for yourself.

3 **DOING THINGS TO PLEASE OTHERS** – Of course you need to show love to the people around you by taking care of them when they need it. But you shouldn't make life decisions to make other people happy. You only have one life to live – do it for yourself.

4 **COMPARING YOURSELF TO OTHERS** – Former US president Theodore Roosevelt once said that 'comparison is the thief of joy' and, boy, was he spot on. Every time you compare yourself to another person, you devalue either them or yourself.

5 **PROCRASTINATING** – Remember all those things you said you would do when you had the time? Why don't you stop planning and just start? It's usually a lack of confidence that stops us attacking our goals head on. We would rather fall at the first hurdle than risk failing in front of others. You will never run out of excuses, but you might run out of time.

6 **LOOKING TO OTHERS TO MAKE US HAPPY** – When you look to others to make you happy, it means that you're not being true to yourself. You convince yourself that you just need to be with those you love to fulfil you, but in truth, we need to be very clear about who we are and what we want in this life. Don't be afraid to own your dreams. If your people love you, they'll be beside you every step of the way.

ALGEBRA FOR LIFE

Life will knock you down, and challenges will come your way. People will hurt or disappoint you. You will have every right to feel angry or to give up. But here's a little home truth for you:

Your reality is your responsibility.

You're probably learning equations and algebra in school, right? And I bet you're wondering if you'll ever actually use them in real life. (TBH, probably not – I certainly never have.) But we have found one very special equation from author Jack Canfield that you can use every single day in every decision, every challenge and every conversation. It's very simple. Are you ready?

$$E + R = O$$

Event + Response = Outcome

Let's start with the **EVENT**. This is the thing that happens to you: rumours spread around school, your parents argue or your ligament tears the day before the county final. Bummer, eh? You can't control the event. Sometimes it comes out of nowhere, and sometimes you see it coming, but no matter what you do, you can't stop it.

The good news is that you can control the next bit: your **RESPONSE**. You, and you alone, can decide what you do in reaction to the event. That, my friend, means that you get to write the ending to your own story.

Confused? Sorry about that. Let's take an example:

Event: You didn't get picked for the school hockey team. You're gutted.

This is where you have choice and control. There are a couple of ways to react here:

RESPONSE 1: *Tell yourself you're a failure, give up hockey, never play again.*

OUTCOME 1: Your confidence takes a battering, and you decide not to take risks or push yourself for fear of disappointment. This rule controls the rest of your life.

RESPONSE 2: *Pick yourself up and dust yourself off. Ask the coach what you could have done differently, take their feedback and work harder.*

OUTCOME 2: Invest another year, more determined than ever, and blow them all away next year.

The situation itself won't have changed, but your perception of it has. Whichever path you choose will have a huge impact on the person you become through the experience.

So there you have it: when life gets real with you, get real about your life, and you will never feel powerless again.

HEY – MAKE YOUR BED!

One small but mighty thing you can do every single day that can transform your life is to make your bed every morning.

Sure, there are loads of excuses not to:

+ I'd rather just have the extra five minutes in bed.

+ It'll just be unmade again later when I get back in.

+ If I leave it, Mom might make it.

+ No one is going to see it today anyway.

Okay, we hear you, valid points indeed. But hear us out. A quick pillow plump and duvet shake will take you two minutes, tops. And there are so many benefits!

IT STARTS YOUR DAY ON THE RIGHT FOOT

And starting your day on the right foot sets the tone for the rest of the day. In his commencement speech at the University of Texas in 2014 (look it up), US Admiral William McRaven said:

'If you make your bed every morning, you will have accomplished the first task of the day. It will give you a small sense of pride, and it will encourage you to do another task and another and another. By the end of the day, that one

task completed will have turned into many tasks completed, Making your bed will also reinforce the fact that little things in life matter.'

I tried it, and you know what? It really does work.

IT ENCOURAGES YOU TO KEEP THE WHOLE ROOM TIDY

Even if your entire floor is covered in socks, tanning mitts and shoes, if your bed is made it's an instant improvement. Maybe when you start with the bed, you'll be inspired to pick up some of the other clutter. Before you know it, you've organised your whole wardrobe.

Your bedroom should be your safe place, your sanctuary. Try your best to keep it Zen-like, and not so zoo-like.

IT MAKES YOU MORE PRODUCTIVE

You might not believe this – it's just a bed, right? Well, yes, it is only a bed. But starting one good habit can kick-start a chain of other good habits and decisions, which can help you to feel more in control of your life. And that in turn increases your wellbeing and overall happiness. All because you took two minutes to pull up your duvet? Yes, indeed.

So start making your bed and before you know it your life will be transformed. (Probably. Okay, maybe.) You can thank us later!

WHERE WILL YOU PUT YOUR ENERGY TODAY?

Every day is a new start, a chance to start over. The best thing we can do is to start every morning by letting go and forgiving ourselves for mistakes we might have made yesterday in order to bounce back and start again.

In order to do that, you need to not worry about:

+ What people think

+ Trying to be cool

+ Needing to know everything

+ Feeling scared

+ The pressure to be perfect

+ Feeling like you have to be always busy to be important

+ Thinking you have no power or control over your own life.

Here are some good alternatives to think about:

+ Doing things that are important to you

+ Being kind to yourself

+ Dancing, laughing and hugging

+ Being creative

+ Sitting quietly and feeling calm

+ Focusing on things you are grateful for.

So where are you going to put your energy today? Are you going to let fear hold you back, or are you going to approach this day with confidence and positivity?

THE POWER OF 'YET'

If there's one word you should add to your vocabulary, it's 'yet'. 'Yet' turns giving-up sentences into goals. See for yourself. Instead of:

+ 'I don't know how to speak French.'

+ 'I can't do fishtail plaits.'

+ 'I don't understand algebra.'

Say:

+ I don't know how to speak French ... yet.'

+ 'I can't do fishtail plaits ... yet.'

+ 'I don't understand algebra ... yet.'

It's amazing what adjusting your language and your attitude just a little bit can do. Never give up on something because it seems tricky or difficult. Stick with it and you'll get there eventually.

Just look at Jim Carrey, who was booed off stage for seven years before his career took off, or Beyoncé, who spent eight years trying to get Destiny's Child together, or Katy Perry, who was dropped by three labels before she had a hit, or even Oprah, who was fired for being 'unfit for TV'!

THE WORD 'PERFECT'

What's your least favourite word? There are a few that make us wince, such as:

Moist …
Fab …
Orifice …
Methinks …

But there's one word in particular that we think should be scratched from the vocabulary of all of us women. That word is:

Perfect

Why do we girls feel under so much pressure to be perfect? Perfect bodies, perfect exam results, perfect friends, perfect relationships, perfect careers, perfect butts and perfect eyebrows.

Every single one of us will fail. Every. Single. One. Because none of us will ever be perfect. It doesn't matter how hard we try; we will never get there. Isn't it enough to just try our best and for our best to be enough? Some days our best will be amazing, and some days our best will mean that we managed to hang in there and put one foot in front of the other. Can't we all see that we need to be OUR best and not THE best? Can we strive to be resilient, hardworking, self-aware and kind?

Ask any adult in your life if they've got it all figured out yet. Chances are they'll say no. Nobody has all the answers, but we can accept and love ourselves just as we are. We are all enough.

When you get older and your back is aching, and you have to get up seven times in the night to pee, you'll look back at who you are now and wish you'd been more accepting of yourself, eaten that extra slice of cake, run into the sea in that bikini and shown yourself some love.

Once more for the people at the back! **YOU. ARE. ENOUGH.**

IT'S OKAY TO MAKE MISTAKES

So you've messed up, eh? Oh dear ...

There's not a person on earth who hasn't royally messed up at least once up in their lives. It's called being human. Maybe you broke a

friend's trust, hurt someone's feelings or made a huge mistake at work. And now you feel like crap.

You lie awake at night replaying the situation over and over again in your head. You know in your heart that you're better than this, but at this moment you feel like the world's worst person.

Beating yourself up isn't doing anyone any good. You need to forgive yourself … or at least *try* to forgive yourself. It's okay to feel guilty as it does serve a purpose, just like every other emotion does. Your mistake can help you become a better person, if you let it. Feeling guilty happens when you have strong values, standards and beliefs. You feel guilty because you crossed your own line. And you know what you need to do to fix it.

To move on, first you need to admit your mistake. Being in denial or acting defensively will only make it worse. Say sorry to whoever you might have hurt, and mean it. Don't demand forgiveness straight away. Make peace with the fact that you may never get it. Give the person space if they need it.

Here comes the most important bit: you need to forgive yourself, and you need to learn how to do better.

This mistake won't define you, unless you make it again, and maybe even again and again. You're not a bad person; you just did a bad thing. **OWN IT.**

HOW TO STEP OUT OF YOUR COMFORT ZONE

The comfort zone is a toasty, snuggly, lovely place to live. Why would anyone ever want to leave? We humans really don't like change. We want to know who's who and what's what at all times. Predictability is good! Why try new things when the old ones suit us just fine?

Well, outside your comfort zone is where you will find your passions, learn new things, accomplish your goals and get to know who you really are and what you're capable of. That's why!

So why do we stay all snug in our cosy little comfort zone? Because leaving it can take a whole lot of effort and, well, can you be bothered?

To push yourself out into the world, you need a bit of motivation. Here are three reasons why you need to kiss the comfort zone goodbye:

1 **IT STOPS YOU GROWING** – You're either moving towards your destiny or away from it. Even if you stand still, time keeps ticking, so you've got to keep up. The world changes constantly, and opportunities will pass you by. Each step towards the future can inspire and empower you to take the next. Stop focusing on what you aren't, and start imagining what you could be.

2 **IT'S KEEPING YOU FROM YOUR PASSIONS** – When you find your passion, it makes you come alive in a way you've never known.

If you're lucky, you'll find it early in life, but you may have to try new things and put yourself out there. We know for a FACT that your passion is not in your comfort zone. And, no, TikTok is not your passion, unless you invented Snapchat. Nice try, pal.

3   IT MAKES IT EASY TO SETTLE – Better the devil you know than the devil you don't, right? Wrong. It's always easy to put up with what you have in your job or your relationships. And that's why we settle. But when you settle you're less likely to take a chance or an opportunity. The more opportunities for happiness the universe throws at you, the more you bat them right back. Eventually, the universe will stop trying.

So what next?

Change something small, and once you start seeing results, more changes will come, and they won't seem so scary.

LET'S GET EXCITED ABOUT LIFE'S CHALLENGES

—

'Being challenged in life is inevitable. Being defeated is optional.'
ROGER CRAWFORD

From learning to tie our shoelaces to an unexpected worldwide pandemic, challenges are a part of all our lives. Generally, we tend to avoid them as they make us feel uncomfortable, but every problem brings life lessons and opportunities. They're not always obvious, but they're always there.

We need to see challenges in a more positive way and to look at the opportunities they bring to learn new things, build our confidence and help us to grow as humans. When you look back at your life, you'll realise that these challenges, and your attitude to them, were the points in your life that formed you as a kind, smart, strong and capable individual.

Challenges will come, so we need to stop running away from them and instead run straight at them with clear heads and full hearts.

Let's look at two of the most common causes of stress for us as young women: **SCHOOL** and **FRIENDSHIPS**. Both can bring huge challenges, but if you can figure out how to navigate them by working through the tough times, you'll be much better prepared for the future. Because school teaches us how to manage in the workplace and friendships prepare us for future relationships, these challenges will show you how to stand up for yourself, communicate with confidence and become a leader.

What to do when a challenge arrives:

1 **DON'T PANIC –** Your body and your mind may scream at you to run away as fast as your legs can carry you. Wait – hold up. Take a breath.

2 **THINK –** You need to understand what the problem is before you can come up with the solution. You may feel overwhelmed, and feeling overwhelmed can lead to anxiety. And that in turn can stop you from thinking clearly.

3 WHAT ARE THE FACTS? What do you know for sure, and what are you overthinking and imagining? Write it all down if you need to, and draw a line under the things you know to be true.

4 ASK YOURSELF THESE THREE QUESTIONS: Is this a real threat? Is it a temporary problem? Can something good come from it? Once you've answered these three questions, you can take back control of the situation.

You may feel like there's a huge mountain ahead of you and think that you could never reach the other side. But do you know what you can do?

Take one step. See? Easy.

And then take another.

Always remember that you are stronger and more capable than you even know.

And that there are always sunny days ahead.

HOW TO STAY CALM UNDER PRESSURE

Steph Golds is a valued member of the Shona team. She is a counselling psychotherapist who has spent countless hours working with young girls. We asked for her advice on staying calm when the world keeps spinning.

There is a lot of scary or stressful information swirling around out there at the moment. It can be easy to get swept along with the tide of panic or to develop your own internal panic, which isn't a nice feeling. We've come up with some tips to help with stress and worry. What's really great about them is that they apply to any scenario that worries you. So have a read and stick them in your toolkit.

WIRED FOR SAFETY

Our brains are designed to keep us safe. When we come into contact with a situation (or information about a situation), we assess what that means for us and respond accordingly. If we see the situation or information as threatening to us, our brain will send a signal to our nervous system, telling it to fire up so that we can survive. A fired-up nervous system feels like panic, which isn't pleasant, but it is a valid response. However, it's important to look back on how we assessed the situation, because that's what sent the signal to the brain in the first place.

FACTS

When we are in the assessment phase, we need facts. Find reliable sources with truthful and professional information. Did you look for all the facts, or was it hearsay? Did you ask questions to clear up any uncertainty? Did you google it? Did you jump on social media and come across scare-posts? The information we take in will directly affect our response.

BREATHING

Notice your breath. Is it shallow – high up in your chest and collarbone area? Or is it deeper – in your rib-cage area? Or deeper still – in the tummy? Shallow breathing engages the nervous system. Deep breathing disengages the nervous system and allows us to relax. That's why everyone says 'take a deep breath', because it really does work! Take two or three minutes, put both feet on the ground, close your eyes and direct your breath – fully in and fully out – and feel the panic start to melt away. When we direct our breath, we can direct our mind.

IRRATIONAL TO RATIONAL

When we are in a state of panic or anxiety, our brain is in an irrational place and we're not able to make clear decisions. Along with deep breathing, there is another way of moving our brain from irrational back to rational again: by doing something with our hands. This is a proven method, and you don't have to be an artist! Here are some suggestions: jigsaws, crosswords, bracelet-making, baking, sketching, writing, knitting, colouring, scrapbooking, playing with a pet, playing an instrument … the list goes on. Find what works for you.

HELP AND SEEK HELP

If you are panicking, find someone who isn't. We often seek out people who are responding in the same way as us, but if you want to reduce panic, find someone who looks calm. And if you're the calm person, find someone who might be panicking and help them. We're all in this thing together.

HOW TO KEEP CALM AROUND EXAM TIME

Exams are stressful. There's no getting around that. We've all had that feeling of being afraid to fall asleep the night before an exam in case everything you've learned falls out of your brain during the night. We also know that guilty feeling you experience when you take a break or a well-needed and well-deserved day off.

The whole exams process involves not just one but two sets of skills. The first, obviously, is studying and learning the information. The second, which is just as important, involves getting all that information onto the page, keeping track of time, crafting good answers and knowing how to strategically pick up those gorgeous extra points.

Have you ever spent 90 minutes writing an amazing essay in an exam only to realise that it's worth just 20 per cent of the marks and that you've run out of time to answer the rest?

Most of us would prefer to trim the lawn with nail scissors than knuckle down to a few hours' study. Let's be honest, we are more likely to spend two hours wondering what our death-row meal would be, organising our sock drawer or practising TikToks. We then convince ourselves that we got some top-quality study done, when in reality it amounted to about 11 minutes in total.

There are only so many brain cells that can be burned in a single sitting, so here's how to make the most of your study time:

1 **SET YOURSELF A SECTION-TARGET INSTEAD OF A TIME-TARGET** – Instead of scheduling two hours, schedule two chapters. That way, you can reward yourself if you finish early with a couple of episodes of *Drag Race*, and you're less inclined to stare at the cracks in the ceiling.

2 **TAKE SHORT BUT REGULAR BREAKS** – Your brain can fire on all cylinders for 45–60 minutes. After that, just stand up, stretch, run up and down the stairs or get a hug from your ma, and then jump back in.

3 **SWITCH OFF PROPERLY WHEN YOU FINISH UP FOR THE NIGHT** – The break times are as important as the work times, as they replenish you for the next day.

4 **MAKE A STUDY PLAYLIST** – If you find silence uncomfortable but find music with lyrics distracting, why not try classical music? Classical music is great to study to, but it's also great at helping with stress. YouTube and Spotify have hundreds of playlists, but I love Ludovico Einaudi and soundtracks from *The Leftovers* or *The Piano*.

5 **TALK TO YOURSELF** – Say it out loud or, better still, make up little songs or jingles. These are especially good for definitions and maths theorems.

6 **FIGURE OUT YOUR MOST PRODUCTIVE TIME** – Are you an early bird or a night owl? If you're a morning person, don't bother trying to pull a late one. Just go to bed and set your alarm for daybreak.

7 ARE YOU READY FOR THE TOPPEST TOP TIP OF ALL TIME? USE MINDMAPS! Our ambassador Megan (you'll meet her again later) said, 'One of my lecturers in college was always banging on about mindmaps, but I didn't really believe him until I gave them a go. Apparently, we remember more of what we see visually in a drawing or diagram than we do in plain text. Over the next four years I became a mindmap ninja. I can't recommend them enough.'

Here's how you create mindmaps:

1 Go to your local pound shop and pick up a lovely selection of highlighter pens or colours (this is the fun bit).

2 Get a blank page, pick a section or chapter and write the heading in the centre of the page.

3 Dot the subheadings around the page, and write in keywords, dates, definitions or descriptions. Just the bits you need to know by heart. You can put them in circles, use bullets, hearts or little stars – go nuts!

4 Keep your words to a minimum, but each one should act as a trigger around which you can write a whole answer.

5 Highlight the sections using highlighters or different coloured lines, emojis or doodles (this is the other fun bit).

6 Draw and redraw the mindmap until you can do it perfectly every time.

7 Narrow your notes down to five or six mindmaps for the entire exam, and know them inside out, upside down and back to front.

ON EXAM DAY:

1 Read the entire exam paper, pick the questions you want to answer and draw your mindmaps on rough-work pages. Now you can relax because you know you've got this.

2 Now all you need to do is structure your answers around your mindmaps.

3 Divide your allocated time for each section, with ten minutes to review at the end. Don't get stuck on one section and realise you haven't left enough time at the end.

4 For the last ten minutes, read over the entire paper and complete any sections you didn't have time for. Add in some bullet points if you don't have time for whole paragraphs, which might help you pick up some sneaky points.

5 Finally, don't get stressed. By exam day there's nothing else you can do, and dosser's remorse won't help you now. Take a deep breath. It'll be over before you know it.

DYSLEXIA: WHEN YOUR MIND WORKS DIFFERENTLY

Dyslexia is a learning difference that affects the way the brain processes written and spoken language. It is not laziness, disruptive behaviour or a sign of stupidity. It is the opposite, in fact; dyslexic people are often very smart, creative and resourceful.

Siobhan works in finance in London. She manages huge portfolios worth millions. She is very ambitious, super-smart and hella strong-willed. She also has dyslexia. For so many of those who struggle with dyslexia, school is very challenging and discouraging, and often their confidence gets knocked, so they don't reach their full potential. Siobhan tells us about her experience and offers some advice to fellow dyslexic people.

When did you realise that school was a struggle for you?
In first class we were given nightly spellings to learn and I would spend hours learning them and writing them out repeatedly in red, black and blue ink to help me recall them, but without fail when I was asked a spelling in school the following day, I would get it wrong and the

teacher would punish me by making me stand in the corner. They don't do that any more, thank God!

Can you remember the first time you heard the word 'dyslexia'?

I'd known for a number of years that I was struggling with my education but never knew why. In Ireland in the '80s and '90s the education system wasn't set up to deal with students with learning disabilities, so many of my teachers ignored the signs or simply put it down to laziness, so when I was diagnosed in university at the age of 23, hearing the word 'dyslexia' was a welcome relief.

At any time did you think you weren't good enough to go to college?

I never felt like I wasn't good enough for college. My major obstacle was convincing teachers and lecturers that I was good enough to stay in education.

Tell us about college.

When I arrived in college, my battle got harder and the level of my disability became more apparent. I struggled to get through every year without having to repeat. It took me six years to complete a four-year degree. I decided in fourth year to transfer to a university in Wales, as the college I was attending in Ireland would only offer a pass degree to me as I had failed to pass some exams at the first sitting. It was while I was at university in Wales that I was diagnosed with dyslexia and began to receive the necessary and essential support for my disability. I was given one-on-one sessions with an educational psychologist, received grants for specialist IT software, was given access to class support where someone would take notes for me in lectures, but the most invaluable support was being given extra time to sit exams.

I graduated with honours, and because I graduated with honours I secured a graduate placement with a bank. This simply would not have happened if I had listened to the doubters. Although having dyslexia is certainly an extra hurdle many need to overcome, it is not and never should be an excuse either for yourself or for our educators to turn a blind eye; but it is down to you to ensure that you receive the best support and that you are never overlooked for opportunities. Never allow educators the opportunity to overlook you because of your disability.

Does your dyslexia affect your work now? How do you deal with that?
Employers have a legal obligation not to discriminate against people with learning disabilities, and in the majority of cases I have found that employers are supportive. I have never shied away or tried to hide my dyslexia from employers, potential employers or clients. I don't believe you ever should.

In terms of day-to-day tasks, yes, there are occasions when my dyslexia is apparent to the outside world, and I often have to reread an email a thousand times before sending it, but that's just how I work with my disability. I accept that I have weaknesses and work harder in those areas, but I celebrate my strengths.

Over the years I have come to embrace it, and in many ways dyslexia has played a major role in making me the person I am today: driven, determined, accepting, tolerant and quirky. I believe people with learning disabilities see the world differently, and that's a unique and special thing.

What advice would you give girls who are currently going through the second-level system? Any hints or tips?

- *If you're struggling, get it checked out. There is always a reason.*
- *Acknowledge that the educational system is only set up with to deal with a standard way of learning. Now, accepting that, find YOUR way of learning. Mindmaps, voice recordings, video classes: there are so many options open to you.*
- *No girl is an island. Seek support and take advantage of all the expert guidance available to you.*
- *Never use it as an excuse not to succeed.*
- *Embrace it, don't fear it, leverage it to drive you forward.*
- *Dyslexia will never hold you back. Only negative attitudes will hold you back.*

WHAT TO SAY INSTEAD OF 'I'M FINE' WHEN YOU'RE NOT FINE

We've all heard the slogan 'It's okay not to be okay.' We see it on posters, Instagram stories and T-shirts, and of course we believe it to be true. So why are we still so slow to ask for help when we need it, instead trying to solve our own problems at a time when we're least able to do so? When asked how we are, we plaster on a smile and say, 'Great, thanks for asking.'

There are a few reasons for this. You may not feel like you are deserving of help; you may not even recognise the problem, and, if you do, you may struggle to put it into words. Or you may not want to burden someone else with your problems. Asking for help can seem like the hardest thing in the world. But sharing how you feel with someone you trust will instantly lighten the load you are carrying, and together you can come up with a solution.

Next time someone you trust asks you how you're doing, and you're not doing well, try responding with one of the following:

1 **'I FEEL LOST, LIKE EVERYTHING IS OUT OF MY CONTROL'** – The irony here is that by naming your feelings, you immediately start to get back some of that control. It's a first step to empowering yourself to get better.

2 **'CAN YOU MAKE AN APPOINTMENT FOR ME?'** – Picking up the phone to call your doctor or a counsellor can feel like a monumental task. Remember that the people who love you want to help. Ask a parent or friend to make the call for you. All you need to think about for now is getting there.

3 **'I FEEL OVERWHELMED'** – This tells your support systems that you've got more on your plate than you can handle right now. You might need to talk through it and break tasks into smaller steps so you can focus on one at a time.

4 **'CAN WE CANCEL OUR PLANS AND STAY IN?'** – Never feel ashamed of needing this. If you constantly cancel plans with friends, they may think that you're a little flakey. Explain that you're doing your best. You may have had every intention of going out but then realised that you need to be where you feel safe. When they understand, they will support you. Remind them that you still appreciate being asked.

5 'THIS IS NOT A GOOD DAY FOR ME' – You may not know what you need, or what will help, but you know that this is a bad day, and you need a little bit of support. There doesn't need to be a reason or a solution. It just is what it is, and it will pass.

6 'DO YOU MIND IF WE CHAT OVER TEXT INSTEAD OF CALLING?' – This is huge for some people, as talking in person or on the phone can be a trigger for anxiety. But you may not want to be completely isolated either. Social media gets a bad rap, but in cases like this it can be a lifeline.

7 'I COULD USE A LITTLE COMPANY' – Depression and anxiety can be very isolating and make you want to be alone. A quick coffee or watching a movie in silence with friends or family might be enough to boost your mood a little.

8 'CAN YOU MAKE SURE I WAKE UP IN TIME?' – Depression can make you feel exhausted, and your body can crave sleep. If you're stressed about sleeping in and missing school or appointments, ask someone to wake you. That's one less thing to worry about.

9 'I'M STRUGGLING WITH SELF-CARE' – Self-care is not all bubblebaths and face-masks. Depression can make showering or taking meds feel like overwhelming tasks. Can you ask someone to help you organise yourself?

10 Remember, asking for help is a sign of strength and integrity. You would never give up on someone you love. Don't give up on yourself.

If you need more help, go and see your GP, who will help you to make a plan.

WHY ASKING FOR HELP SAVED MY LIFE

Amelia shares her story about going through a tough time and how she learned the importance of asking for help when coping with depression.

When I was 16, my parents separated, and the world as I knew it fell apart. To say that my mental health suffered is an understatement. I went from being the overachieving athlete who was comfortable and confident in her body to an anxious, isolated person who struggled to interact with the outside world.

I started to lock myself in my room for days on end, sitting in the dark and crying for hours and hours. I convinced myself that every bad thing that had ever happened was my fault and went over and over all my actions and decisions trying to come up with ways I could have stopped it.

Of course, none of it was my fault. I know that now.

I was diagnosed with clinical depression, and shut everyone out, including my mother, the one person who loved me the most. I didn't want to see or talk to anyone, and stopped even reading my text messages. I stopped training, the one thing that had always defined who I was. I believed I was nobody.

Day after day, week after week, month after month, I sank further and further. I felt empty, worthless and hopeless.

One day, for no reason I can think of, out of nowhere, the fog cleared just enough for me to see that the world was going on without me. My friends were having fun, laughing and enjoying life. And there I was, stuck in my room, missing out on what were supposed to be the best years of my life.

That's when I knew I needed to ask for help. My mother was overjoyed, she thought everything was going to be okay, but it wasn't that simple. Recovery isn't a straight line. She lined me up with a counselling appointment, but I quit straight afterwards. I didn't believe that anyone would understand how I felt or that anyone could help me. I was wrong.

To keep my mam happy, I went back for a second appointment, and that's when it clicked. I went twice a week for two years, and even came to look forward to it. If anything bothered me during the week, I would park it for counselling, and know that I'd have the space and the tools to figure it out at my next session.

A problem shared is a problem halved.

I've never been 'cured' of my depression. It's a condition that I have to manage, but counselling has given me lots of tools that I still use. I can identify triggers and panic points and talk myself into dealing with the facts without going straight to catastrophe as I used to.

My mental health issues were stopping me being my whole self, from achieving all the things I wanted and deserved. It was time for a change. Asking for help was the start of a new life.

Over the years, I have gone back to counselling when I need to. I also learned about Cognitive Behavioural Therapy (CBT), which taught me methods and breathing techniques I still use all the time.

I am now 20 and still struggle at times, but I have an amazing mom, sister and boyfriend who know, understand and love me. They always help me through it. I have never felt happier or more content. I am finally comfortable in my own skin, I like who I am!

Remember, we are all works in progress. You grow through what you go through. Your story is yours to write. If you need help, ask for it. Take it from me.

WE NEED TO TALK ABOUT SELF-HARM

Self-harm is unfortunately an issue that we need to have an honest and open conversation about. As usual, our go-to when it comes to the big stuff, Steph Golds, is on hand. Having worked with teenage girls for quite some time, she really sees how self-harm can affect our lives. Here she explains the topic of self-harm to us in more detail.

Self-harm is quite common among the teenage population, in particular girls, and in particular in Ireland. In 2018, we had our highest number of hospital presentations for self-harm since 2002. We also have the highest rate in Europe of girls taking their own lives. And there are even more girls who don't present to hospitals, who suffer in silence. This is something we really need to talk about.

The term 'self-harm' seems contradictory – that the self would be harmed by the self – but it happens, at an alarming rate. There are young girls, across our country, hurting themselves every day. Why? Because they're in pain, for different reasons and due to different life events. They're hurting and for some reason they either can't or don't want to express it.

So what kind of things might trigger this type of pain? Lots of things. Stress at home, or at school, death of a loved one, rejection by a friend or family member, unwanted life transitions like moving house or school, parental breakdown, bullying, confusion about identity, a medical diagnosis, a traumatic childhood, an ill parent, the list goes on.

Painful life experiences bring up lots of emotion within us – fear, sadness, loneliness, anger, rage, resentment, disappointment, guilt, shame, self-hatred – and when we aren't able to address the experience and/or the emotion, our psyche will find another way to cope with it. When we keep big emotions like that to ourselves, an internal pressure builds up inside us, and it will look for an outlet. It's like a river – it will find a way out eventually, even if it has to reroute. Self-harm becomes a way of coping; it releases that pressure that builds up when we don't speak up. The problem is that although self-harm *feels* like it is relieving pressure, it is actually just kicking the can down the road. Self-harm provides temporary relief but it doesn't provide any real help and it doesn't improve the situation. It's a short-term solution that attacks our deepest self, so we need more productive, long-term solutions.

Forms of self-harm include cutting, burning, skin-picking, hair-pulling, drug and alcohol abuse, digital self-harm, and self-criticism. Digital self-harm occurs when someone engages in destructive activity and even slags themselves off online. Our harsh inner voice can also be a form of self-harm. Many of us speak to ourselves with a spiteful vindictiveness that would take your breath away if we spoke this way to anyone else. With all kinds of self-harm the result is the same; the person feels relieved, momentarily. It's like opening a fizzed-up bottle – it releases the pressure and then everything settles. Self-harm is interesting in that it tends to be a private and secretive ritual, but it can also be a very visual expression of pain for the world to see. It's a form of communication, similar to eating disorders, where the internal pain is trying to come to the surface to be recognised, accepted, validated, and then healed. But rather than coming to the surface in words, or even tears, it comes in cuts, and burns, and bruises, and bodies that need lots of tender loving care.

Self-harm is an understandable response to pain. And while it's not healthy or helpful in the long run, it can appear to provide an outlet for someone whose world has become chaotic. People who engage in self-harm have a desire to hurt and a desire to be hurt. Self-harm damages our inner psyche and exacerbates our critical inner voice, and it often leads us to become even more filled with self-loathing.

If you or someone you know is self-harming, understanding purpose is crucial. When we understand the purpose of things, we can start to look for new, more helpful ways of coping. There are lots of people and organisations around this little country of ours who can help. They might not understand your exact situation, but they can listen. They want to listen. We're all ready to listen. Because we love you.

WHAT THERAPY IS REALLY LIKE

Niamh is a Shona ambassador, and she very kindly shared her experience of personal therapy with us. Trying anything for the first time can be daunting, so hearing from someone like Niamh might help to put your mind at ease.

Recently, I attended my first personal therapy session, so I wanted to share my experience with all you lovely ladies. I want to let anyone who is struggling know that it's okay not to be okay (cliché) and that reaching out for help is really brave! This post isn't going to be about me and my first therapy session. It's going to be for others who might not know where to start and it will hopefully act as a guide if they think they might need personal therapy.

First of all, what exactly is therapy?
Well, individual therapy involves you sitting down one-on-one with a therapist and talking about whatever you want to talk about. Therapy can provide you with a safe space to let out some thoughts and untangle some messy things that might be going on in your head. Therapists are trained to listen in a non-judgemental and non-directive way. This means that they won't be able to tell you exactly what to do or provide you with all the answers. Instead they allow you to explore your own thought processes and come to your own conclusions, with some subtle guidance.

How do I know if I need therapy?

See below ...

In all seriousness, if something is bothering you, no matter how big or small, it might benefit you to talk to someone who is trained to listen. You might think nobody will understand, or that your problems are insignificant or that you don't 'need' therapy, or you're too proud to go to therapy, or therapy is only for 'crazy' people. Therapists have seen it all and will be eager to help anyone who walks in their door. We all deserve to be happy and to be our best selves, and we all deserve therapy if we feel we need it.

How do I see a therapist?

There are two routes you can choose. The first route is the public route, and this involves a visit to your GP. Your GP can make a referral for you to see somebody (they'll know what/who is available in your area) and this is funded through the HSE (free). The second route is the private route, and this means that you see somebody in a private practice and you pay for this yourself. Typically, a one-on-one session will cost you anywhere between €40 and €70. But don't freak out, it doesn't always have to be super expensive. Some therapists will offer a sliding scale, and this means that you pay based on what you can afford (phew!), so it's always worth asking about this. Also, many schools, colleges and universities provide free counselling services, so do look into this.

How do I know what therapist to choose?

Finding the right therapist to work with is a really individual process, and what works for some might not work for others. It can be a bit of a trial and error process, but don't let this discourage you – it might just take some time to find out what works best for you. First of all, make sure they are accredited! Different therapists take different approaches, such as psychodynamic, CBT, person-centred and many more. Just do a bit of googling to find out what each therapy is about and have a think about whether it might suit you. Many therapists will be trained in many disciplines and will often adapt to what works for you as you progress.

What's the first session like?

You and the therapist will sit in a room together where you will be free to discuss whatever is on your mind. All therapy rooms look different, some might have a couch, some might have a single armchair, some might be dimly lit, some might be brighter. It might be a room in someone's house, it might be a private office in a clinic, it might be nicely decorated, or it might not be to your taste. No two will be the same.

In your first session, the therapist will usually lay out the 'contract'. This is just so you know how the sessions work. The first session will be different for everyone. For some, nothing too heavy is discussed in the first session, and it can be like a settling-in session. Others may want to jump straight in and get to the good stuff. It's up to you and the therapist to work this out. It's so, so important that you feel comfortable with your therapist and that you feel you can trust them. If you don't feel these things, it's unlikely that you'll make much progress. If you feel you don't 'click', that's okay. You can politely let them know that you're not sure this is the right therapy for you and move on (they won't be offended, I promise). Sometimes the therapist will take some brief notes, and this is nothing to worry about, it's just for their own records so they can keep track of how you're doing. The sessions will usually last 45–60 minutes.

Some last points:
- *You might cry*
- *You don't have to lie down on a couch like they make out on TV and films (but feel free to do so if you wish)*
- *It's not always all about childhood trauma*
- *It might not be easy*
- *It doesn't have to be for ever*
- *There is no shame in going to therapy.*

ON AUTISM

Ciara-Beth would really love people to better understand autism. This is why she has shared her story.

Disclaimer: This article is based on personal experiences. I speak only about my own experiences; the experiences of others may differ.

I have always been different. Different enough that it was noticeable, but not so different that people felt bad about treating me poorly. While most teenagers and young adults have trouble with relationships, school, family life or all of the above, autism definitely creates unique problems within these categories.

These are the things I wish you knew about me, an autistic girl.

I like to feel included

There aren't many people who don't like feeling included. I never much liked parties or going out, but I always appreciate it when someone invites me anyway. While I may not accept the invitation, I always appreciate it, because it means that the person likes having me around. Making and maintaining friendships is a struggle for many people who have autism, even more than your average teen. I will always appreciate someone trying to include me.

Verbal communication isn't always a strong suit of mine

Having a conversation takes a lot of thinking for me. There are so many social rules that come naturally to most, but that I have had to (and still have to) learn. One of my favourite reference texts for social rules is The Asperkid's (Secret) Book of Social Rules, which is a book I think every teen who has autism would benefit from. So if you're talking to me, and I'm taking longer than average to respond, or I start talking about something that is waaaay off-topic, please try to be patient. I promise I am actually doing my best.

Like most young people, I'm self-conscious as it is: you staring doesn't help

Okay, I 100 per cent acknowledge that sometimes I do things that probably look very strange to you. Maybe you don't even realise you're staring at me. Unfortunately, the world isn't fluent in the language of Ciara-Beth. Most people doesn't even know it exists. So if I burst into tears in public and can't communicate verbally, or if I'm flapping my hands or jumping around like a lunatic or wearing an outfit that is DEFINITELY not stylish, just know that it's for a reason. I may be overwhelmed or excited, or I might have woken up this morning feeling like every item of clothing in my wardrobe bar that one dress was making my skin feel like I was burning alive. Staring at me when these things happen make me feel like an idiot, and nobody likes feeling like an idiot.

I'm autistic, not an idiot

If I meet you when I'm out with a friend or a parent, and you find out I have autism and start asking the person who I'm with questions about me or what I want, you're insulting me. Unless I cannot verbally communicate with you (which will be very obvious, I promise), it's rude and disrespectful, to both me and the person I'm with, to talk to the person beside me about me. If you're in doubt, ask me the question, and if I can't communicate, the person who's with me will explain. I promise, you're not making a mistake if you ask me a question and I can't communicate with you.

I always appreciate an attempt to understand me
I have spent 20 years trying to understand how your world works. I might seem like I understand most things, but a lot of social rules just don't make sense to me. All the same, I respect that they make sense to you. If you spend even 10 minutes building Lego with me, or if you're holding an event and you ask me how you can make it accessible for me, I will appreciate it. Any attempt you make to try and make sense of my world will always be welcomed with open arms. And if you accidentally get it wrong, I promise I won't be mad.

So there you have it: five key things I wish everyone could know about me as an autistic girl. I hope my world makes even a slight bit more sense to you.

AsIAm is an amazing organisation that provides information, advice and support. Check them out at asiam.ie

COMMUNICATION: DO YOU GET ME?

Listen up! (See what we did there?) This might sound like a really obvious point, but if you want to have deep and long-lasting friendships, or have a relationship that's not full of arguments or get ahead in school, in your career and in life in general, you need to learn how to **COMMUNICATE**.

Communicating is not just about being able to TALK so people understand, it's also about being able to LISTEN so YOU understand.

Do you ever find yourself in a conversation thinking so hard about what to say next that you've not heard a word the other person has said? Or maybe it's the other way around and you keep all your own feelings and thoughts inside because you don't believe they have value? (Spoiler alert – of course they do!)

Remember that everyone wants to feel heard, including you. When you nail that, the real, meaningful relationships can be made. And that's the good stuff. In relationships, disagreements often happen when both people have different viewpoints, and each just can't explain or understand where the other is coming from. We focus way too much on winning the argument, rather than solving the problem. When this happens, ask yourself: do I want to be right? Or do I want to be happy?

So here are the basics.

Communication can take three different forms: **PASSIVE, AGGRESSIVE** and **ASSERTIVE**.

+ **PASSIVE COMMUNICATION** happens when you give someone else the upper hand in the conversation. You just absorb what they have to say and don't consider your own opinions, needs or feelings.

+ **AGGRESSIVE COMMUNICATION** happens when you only care about what you have to say and don't have any interest in listening to the other person. You may even interrupt or shout over them.

+ ASSERTIVENESS is where the sweet spot is. You say your piece, and then you listen to theirs. You both listen, understand and respect each other's points. And then you either try to find a compromise, or agree to disagree.

Here are a few communication hacks you can practise before you announce you're running for president.

+ USE THE WORD 'I' as much as you can. As in 'I feel' or 'I need'.

+ AVOID TRYING TO SORT OUT A PROBLEM OVER TEXT – If you can't meet in person, try to at least FaceTime. This is important because ...

+ EYE CONTACT helps the other person get all that gorgeous non-verbal communication through your body language.

+ HOLD YOUR HEAD UP – Don't apologise for having an opinion.

+ BE CLEAR – Instead of saying, 'Emmm, I dunno about that,' say, 'I don't really want to do that, but thank you.'

+ WATCH YOUR TONE – Don't shout, but equally, don't whisper. Speak with confidence but not aggression.

HOW TO LISTEN

Listening is not just about hearing words. It's about hearing, thinking, understanding and respecting. There's an easy, cool little hack that can help with this too. It's called 'reflection'. All you need to do is repeat back what the person has said in your own words. For example, when your sister says, 'School is so stressful. I'm just so moody when I get home,' you say, 'I hear ya, school is stressing you out, so you're exhausted and frustrated after a whole day of it?'

Listen, this sounds obvious, but it really makes a difference, and we all need reminders sometimes. Just try it and see!

MY STORY: ABIGAIL

—

SOCIAL ANXIETY

—

Abigail is a Shona ambassador, and a powerful advocate for mental health. She is passionate about the importance of minding ourselves, and taking time to heal when we need it.

I've always struggled to explain the personality I have. When I'm out in a group of friends or family, I feel like an extrovert. I can be loud and chatty and funny (if I do say so myself). I feel comfortable in large groups, and I do enjoy going out and having fun. However, when I'm at home, or when people ask to meet up or make plans, it takes a lot of energy and motivation for me to get up and be involved. I love going out, and I rarely regret it, it just takes a lot for me to get there. I used to think my behaviour was antisocial, but I kept saying to myself, No, I want to be around people, I want to have fun. I just can't get myself to get out of the house at times.

The past few months have been really hard for me. I've become quite a busy person during the past couple of years: I'm involved in different mental health organisations, working four to five days a week and a full-time college student. Unfortunately for me, my social battery doesn't last long. A full day of work leaves me drained from all the interaction, and if anyone asks me to meet up afterwards, I feel like I physically can't. Of course, I'm always so busy on purpose. I love keeping busy and wouldn't have it any other way, but sometimes I wish I could have more energy and motivation for my personal social life. Missing out on plans with friends due to my lack of motivation or energy doesn't help with my mental health. It's a bit of a vicious circle. I stay in and miss plans to make myself feel better and more comfortable. But then missing fun nights out and enjoying myself makes me feel down and disappointed in myself.

For weeks I've been apologising to friends for my behaviour, for not interacting as much as I should, for missing out on plans. I know I shouldn't have to do this as they're my friends. They love me regardless, but the paranoia that everyone hates me for missing out is sometimes too much.

I've been doing some research to see if my behaviour is normal and I came across the word 'asocial'. Asociality refers to the lack of motivation to engage in social interaction, or a preference for solitary activities, not to be confused with antisocial behaviour. An asocial person's behaviour is not due to their lack of social skills but rather their fear of ridicule, embarrassment or a lack of self-confidence. I started reading more into this, and it turns out asociality is prevalent with people who suffer from depression and anxiety. And at that moment I felt relieved.

I realised that I am not the only person who has ever behaved or felt like this, and this doesn't define me. Suffering from depression makes you lose interest in or motivation for partaking in activities you might have loved at one time. My depression can be fine at times but still hits me hard every so often. Sometimes I forget that I still suffer from this illness. I shouldn't be so hard on myself. I am learning more and more about myself every day, and I am learning new ways in which I can cope with these obstacles my mental health throws at me. And really, that's all I can do: continue to learn and grow. Hopefully, one day I'll be able to overcome all this social anxiety pent up within me.

For now, I refuse to feel ashamed about taking time for myself to recharge my batteries. Self-care is not selfish. Even though I may need a little more self-care than the 'average' person does, it's crucial for my wellbeing.

101 ANXIETY AND STRESS HACKS

1   Set an alarm for 15 minutes earlier than usual.
2   Get organised the night before.
3   Keep a calendar and schedule your tasks.
4   Write stuff down – don't rely on memory.
5   Get a spare key.
6   Say 'no' sometimes.
7   Make a list of priorities.
8   Avoid negative people.
9   Stop time-wasting.
10 Remember that self-care is not time-wasting.
11 Organise your meals.
12 Back up your documents.
13 Hit the 'save' button more often.

14   Think about what your needs are.

15   Get rid of, or fix, broken stuff.

16   Ask people to help you.

17   Break down big tasks into smaller pieces.

18   Look at your challenges as opportunities.

19   Try to find some positives in your problems.

20   Get rid of clutter.

21   Smile.

22   Carry an umbrella.

23   Listen to the birds.

24   Pet all the dogs you pass.

25   Don't try to have answers to everything.

26   Look for silver linings.

27   Pay someone a compliment.

28   Watch them smile.

29   Fly a kite.

30   Dance in the rain.

31   Stop worrying about your hair.

32   Make time for play.

33   Use that bathbomb you've been saving.

34   Own your choices and decisions.

35   Believe in yourself.

36   Stop beating yourself up.

37   Visualise the future (the good stuff).

38   See the funny side more often.

39   Stop saying 'Everything will be better when ...'

40   Set goals.

41   Allow your goals to change.

42   Dance.

43   Chat to a stranger at the bus stop.

44 Lie on your back and look at the stars.

45 Ask someone you love for a hug.

46 Breathe.

47 Whistle – loudly.

48 Read poetry.

49 Listen to an opera.

50 Read a book curled up in bed.

51 Listen to a podcast.

52 Try something new.

53 Stop a bad habit.

54 Buy yourself flowers.

55 Smell those flowers.

56 Get support when you need it.

57 Get a 'rant buddy'.

58 Stop putting off your dreams.

59 Work on your positivity.

60 Stay safe.

61 Do everything in moderation.

62 Brush your hair.

63 Strive for progress, not perfection.

64 Stretch.

65 Paint a picture.

66 Hum your favourite theme tune.

67 Sit under a tree.

68 Feed the pigeons, or the ducks, or the swans.

69 Touch your toes.

70 Always have a plan B (or C or D).

71 Doodle.

72 Always have a go-to joke.

73 Take responsibility for yourself.

74 Recognise your own needs.

75 Listen more than you talk.

76 Know your limits.

77 Set boundaries.

78 Learn how to say 'Hi' in other languages.

79 Make a paper plane.

80 Move – every day.

81 Learn the lyrics to a rap song in full.

82 Always arrive five minutes early.

83 Clean out your wardrobe.

84 Watch a Disney movie.

85 Have a picnic.

86 Walk more than you need to.

87 Take more days off.

88 Eat popcorn with melted chocolate (trust me).

89 Write an actual letter.

90 Scream loudly.

91 Light a candle.

92 Know the people who really love you.

93 Don't let stress stop you thriving.

94 Keep a journal.

95 Smile (again!).

96 Remember there is always more than one way.

97 Always have a happy place – go there.

98 Don't try to fix everyone else's problems.

99 Get more sleep.

100 Give praise to those who deserve it.

101 Practise gratitude.

WHEN YOUR PANIC ATTACKS HAVE NO CHILL

Alannah suffers from panic attacks. Eighteen months ago, her dad left and her family went through a very stressful time. As a result, she sometimes has a couple of attacks in one week. Here is her story.

In the past twelve months, my life has changed in a way I never thought could happen. I'm one of those people who overthink, but overthink to an extreme. I feel like a different person, not the old me who was full of energy and adventure, dancing and playing football. But all of that seemed to slip through my fingers all too fast. Sometimes it feels like a dream or someone else's old life.

You always hear things that have happened to other families and think, 'God, I don't know what I'd do if that happened in my family.' I actually said that only a month or two before it did happen to my family. My father cheated on my mam, and we found out just a couple of weeks after my grandad passed away. I have never been so angry or helpless in all my life. Before all of this, I had just gained some confidence, and now it was back on the floor.

My house was a misery. Nearly two years on, we are all very different because of it. We don't trust people as easily, and we try not to get upset in front of each other. When I feel anxious, I get really quiet and frustrated at myself. It affects me in ways that I know don't reflect the real me. Tired, crying, a lump in my throat, always afraid of something terrible happening. Overthinking about literally everything.

One of my biggest fears is losing people, the ones who are closest to me. I remember being in an argument with one of my friends, and I wanted to solve it ASAP because the anxiety was killing me. I had three panic attacks that week, I couldn't eat or sleep and I was just emotionally exhausted.

To me, the only way that I can fight anxiety is to talk to someone I trust and get it all out of my head. Anything conflict-related makes it worse, so nip it in the bud IN PERSON, never over text. Keep yourself busy, which leaves less time for your mind to wander. Exercise is great for this. Lastly, be organised, as leaving certain things to the last minute will make you stress even more.

These are my steps for dealing with an anxious day or a panic attack:
- *If you feel a panic attack coming on, get out of whatever surroundings you're in and go somewhere safe.*
- *Cry it all out. Holding it in will make it worse.*
- *Having someone you know, with a calming voice, helps loads. Someone telling you to calm down isn't helpful.*
- *Your thoughts will be going 90 miles an hour, but listen to the person trying to help you breathe.*
- *Knowing that you'll be okay is a comfort, so keep telling yourself that.*
- *Lastly, the main thing is to breathe. Breathe in slowly, hold it for a second, and then breathe out very slowly.*

Alannah said that writing this piece really helped her get her head around what she's been through. She is getting help for her anxiety and panic attacks and knows she'll come through this time in her life stronger. She says, 'In many ways, all of this has changed me as a person, but I like who I am. Knowing I could help someone who feels the same really helped me to write this piece. It frustrates me so much when I see someone in an anxious state or a panic attack, and no one seems to know what to do or how to help.'

7-11 BREATHING

Stress and anxiety are taking over our lives. The world is moving so fast that we struggle to keep up. As a result, we get overwhelmed, and that feeling shows itself through anxiousness and panic. The 7-11 breathing technique is a simple but powerful tool to relax and help you regain control of your breathing. Breathing techniques are not mind tricks. They produce a response that physically lowers your anxiety rate. We love this technique because you can do it anywhere, any time, it's free and it WORKS!

The theory is easy. When you make your out-breath longer than your in-breath, it helps your mind and body to slow down almost immediately. Next time your head starts spinning, go somewhere calm and quiet – even the toilet will do – and practise this for a few minutes.

Here's how, and it is as easy as it sounds:

1 Take a long breath in for a count of 7.

2 Let a long breath out for a count of 11.

When you breathe in, use your diaphragm, filling your belly and lungs with air, instead of just gulping air into your mouth. If 7-11 is too hard, try 3-5, or whatever works, just as long as the out-breath is longer than the in-breath. This is an excellent tool, and although it won't work for everyone it's definitely worth a try.

MY STORY: AOBHA

—

ON INSECURITIES

—

Aobha's insecurities held her back for a long time.
Now she has learned to love herself more.

I can tell you exactly when I first felt insecure. I had just moved to secondary school and was trying to find my way, make new friends and not screw up too badly. One day, a new friend of mine made me laugh loudly and, out of nowhere, a girl I had never met before walked straight up to me and said, 'When you laugh, your nose looks even bigger.' Wow. Just ... wow.

I don't know why she felt I needed to hear that or what she was hoping to achieve, but I was devastated. I felt my cheeks flush with embarrassment, and knowing that I had gone red made me feel even more embarrassed. I was so shocked that I didn't react to her and when she had walked away, I just half-laughed at my friend as if I didn't care and said, 'What's her problem?'

But I did care then, I have cared ever since, and I still care now.

When I was in primary school, I never cared or gave much thought to what I looked like. I loved my unicorn T-shirt and my Marvel pyjamas, but as for my own face and body, I never thought about them. My mother would try to grab me to brush my hair as I ran out the door, or to make sure I put clean socks on, but that was it. I would give anything now to be able to go back to that time when I could run to see my friends or go to a birthday party without worrying what everyone would think of me, whether I looked okay or if I had said anything stupid.

It makes me really sad when I think about how we are judged for how we look. It takes a massive amount of energy to figure out who the world wants us to be, and then to be that. We can't wear too much or too little make-up. Our clothes are too frumpy, or too revealing. It's exhausting! I know it's not just me who struggles – my friends all feel the same. We are under pressure to show our worth by having the coolest clothes or the best eyebrows.

I've learned that to love myself, I need to let that stuff go, to try to focus on the bits of myself that I like and to stop being my own worst critic.

We are the selfie generation, and that's not something that makes me proud. I look at my parents' photo albums and see the fun they had as teens. And those photos are precious to them, even if they have red-eye or the angle isn't flattering, because they capture a moment. I don't even know how many photos I've deleted because the lighting was a little off or because my spots were visible. All those memories I erased because my appearance in them was more important to me than the experience I just had. In years to come, will we look back at those photos and examine our skin? Or will we look at the faces of our friends and feel love and joy? I've made my choice!

SUPERHERO STANCE

Something big coming up? Feeling nervous? We've all had those big 'palms are sweaty, Mom's spaghetti' moments. You've got an entire swarm of butterflies doing the cha-cha in your stomach, and your deodorant has never worked so hard. You're convinced that your nerves are going to prevent you being your best self in this important moment.

But wait! Here's a secret: you can actually trick your body into believing that everything is totally under control and there's nothing to stress about. Standing in a superhero position (also known as a 'power pose') before taking to the stage has been scientifically proven to improve your performance.

Who knew it was so easy?

Studies in Harvard and Columbia universities (fancy!) found that standing in a power pose can boost testosterone and reduce cortisol (the stress hormone – most useful if you need to run from a bear). So if you stand like a superhero and think you're a superhero, you become a superhero. (Just don't try to fly just yet!)

Here are three power poses to try ...

The Superhero
Stand with your feet hip-width apart. Press your fists onto your hips. Stick your chest upwards and outwards. Turn your face to the sky. Hold for two minutes.

The Boss
Sit in your chair with your arms folded back behind your head. Flex your elbows outwards. Stretch your feet out onto the table. Hold for two minutes.

The Decider
Stand facing your desk with your feet hip-width apart and planted firmly on the ground. Lean your hands on the table and push your chest out. Hold for two minutes.

These poses might sound simple, but if they make you feel brave, strong, confident or powerful, why wouldn't you give them a try? Just two minutes? Go for it.

MY EXPERIENCE WITH ANOREXIA

Megan is a Shona ambassador from County Galway, now living in Cork. She has shared her experience with an eating disorder with us a number of times, and we've watched her grow stronger and more powerful over the years.

I can't tell you when it started, because if I did, I would be lying. The truth is, I don't remember. It's all a blur really. What I do know is that there was no cause, no reason why I developed an eating disorder despite numerous doctors questioning me about my past, as if to find an easily explainable reason for my suffering. It is not that simple. My official diagnosis occurred at age 14 only because I was thin enough to be counted as 'an anorexic' at that time. Before my BMI fell below a certain point, no healthcare professional mentioned anything about anorexia, even though I had all the other symptoms. It was only when my BMI was dangerously low that I started to get proper treatment.

It started with being hospitalised, then continued with weekly sessions at a public mental health centre for children and teens. I had to take time off school as life became too hard to handle. I woke up every morning with dreadful thoughts because I knew the terrible battles that lay ahead. Having my mom prepare my breakfast, lunch, dinner and snacks as per my meal plan was terrifying. Every day was the same: sitting down for my routine meals with my heart pounding so much I thought it would stop, crying after eating 'unsafe' foods because I felt like a failure, sitting curled up beside the fire wearing so many layers to keep my bones warm.

When other girls my age started going to discos and house parties, I stayed in my little bubble at home. I would look at them and wonder how they had the confidence to be so sociable, how they could go out dressed up and be happy, while I loathed my body. During this period, I spent a lot of time studying as a way of distraction and ended up getting 10 As in my Junior Cert. Although I was happy with this, I saw it as a sign of how sick I really was, how I spent so much time studying instead of living. I decided it was time to take control of my eating disorder and try my hardest with recovery.

I skipped Transition Year and went straight into fifth year, where I met new friends and improved my confidence. I continued going to my counselling sessions throughout this time. I also tried various other treatment methods, including homoeopathy, reflexology and meditation. Eating became less scary and more enjoyable as I began to eat foods I hadn't eaten in years. I could go for food with friends and be included in occasions involving food.

When the time came for me to decide on my CAO, it was clear to me that I wanted to work in the area of mental health and learn more about people and how their minds work. I studied hard and was lucky to get my first choice to study psychology and sociology in the University of Limerick. I've almost finished my first year there now, and I cannot believe how far I've come. Believe me when I say that recovery from *an eating disorder, along with other mental illnesses, is not a straight road. My journey was, and still is, very bumpy. I have my bad days, but I also have my good ones. I've learned so much through it all, and now I'm a much stronger person than I used to be.*

If I could go back and tell my 13-year-old self something, it would be to embrace who you are, embrace every inch of it, because what you eat does not define who you are. Nor does the shape of your body or the calories you consume. If only I could have known how to love myself at that young age; I wouldn't have to look back on the wasted days of my youth. All the fun, laughter and chats I've missed out on and the friends and family I've hurt. But at least I know that now and can use this knowledge to help other boys and girls struggling with body image and eating disorders.

'I love the person I've become because I've fought to become her.'

NINE THINGS WE GIRLS NEED TO STOP SHAMING EACH OTHER FOR

If we're honest, we girls can be a little judgy, would you agree? Instead of valuing our differences, we compete to be the smartest, the prettiest, the most athletic, the most popular.

When we look in the mirror, we see mostly faults and, for some weird reason, seeing flaws in others makes us feel better. Shame is such a destructive thing, and shaming each other is not okay.

Here are some things we need to stop shaming each other for:

+ **APPEARANCE** – 51 per cent of young people say they've been bullied for how they look. No matter how much we try, we will never please everyone. If you have pink hair, 75 piercings or a tattoo of an armadillo on your face, it's your own business.

+ **SIZE** – Skinny-shaming and fat-shaming are both equally harmful. Your size is no one else's business. Once you respect your body, that's all that matters. Love it because of all the amazing things it allows you to do.

+ **TASTE** – We are all individuals who have different passions, opinions, likes and dislikes. We're also attracted to different people for many different reasons. That's what makes the world go round. If you like headbanging to death metal, while she listens to classical piano, good for you and good for her too!

+ **BEING SINGLE** – In case we haven't been clear before, being in a relationship doesn't make you a whole person or a better person than anyone else. Some people feel that if they're not coupled up, they're not good enough. This is unhealthy, as lots of people would prefer to stay in a destructive relationship than be alone. Not having a romantic partner doesn't mean you are alone. There are many other meaningful relationships with friends and family that can last longer and be more fulfilling. There's way too much pressure on young people to be coupled up. Take your time and have some fun!

+ **NUMBER OF ROMANTIC RELATIONSHIPS** – None of us has any right to assume that we know how many relationships other girls have had and what they did in those relationships. We have no right to judge anyone for their choices. Slut-shaming comes from an unrealistic and outdated view that girls should never be involved in sexual relationships before they get married. Each of us has the right to set her own rules once she has reached an appropriate age, is careful, and respects herself.

+ SEXUALITY – You may like boys, girls or both. And that is entirely your own business. Love is love. End of discussion.

+ MENTAL HEALTH – Historically, people with mental illness were seen as weak or incapable. If you, or someone you know, have to deal with depression or anxiety every day, you will know the strength and determination it takes to ask for help and to fight back again and again. We have so much to learn from those who are struggling with mental health and we should recognise and admire them.

+ FEMININITY – What does a real woman look like? Some are petite and delicate with tiny waists. Some have muscles that could bend iron. Some like to wear high heels and fake eyelashes, and some prefer to live in Converse and never wear make-up. Women look like whatever the hell they want to look like.

+ FAMILY BACKGROUND – Some of us are born lucky, with lives full of support and opportunities. Others start with nothing and have only themselves to rely on to create a future. Those who succeed based on pure determination are smart, strong, and have an incredible capacity for coping with stress. Never judge them for where they came from. Also, many people come from homes where there are no role models. Our family history does not define us. We define ourselves.

IS IT HORMONES OR AM I LOSING MY MIND?

No, you're not crazy. Teenage brains just feel like that sometimes.

The teenage years can feel like an **EMOTIONAL ROLLERCOASTER**. One minute you're happy and the next you're trying to figure out why everyone around you is so damn irritating! This is all perfectly normal. Let me explain.

The stress of fitting in, rowing with your parents and keeping up with homework is real. On top of all of that, adolescent hormones and bodily changes make life so much more complicated. The good news is that your brain is doing what it's supposed to – it's preparing you for adulthood. While it's a rough ride sometimes, it'll all work out in the end.

As teenagers, regulating ourselves isn't easy, which is why we overthink, act impulsively and feel negatively about things. We worry about being smart enough, pretty enough, and successful enough. We feel like we're being judged by everyone, including our parents. It's a LOT to deal with.

As you move from childhood your brain does a clear-out of the bits it doesn't need, holding on to long-term memory, significant experiences, talents and interests. This is called 'synaptic pruning'. Fancy! During this phase, your frontal lobes aren't quite showing up for you. The frontal lobes help you control impulses, consider your situations carefully, make positive decisions and plans, and be a nice person to hang out with. Basically, your brain turns you into a world-class racehorse that's being ridden by a three-year-old.

You're also being bombarded with surges of hormones, which can make you go from chilled out to stressed out in seconds. You can even swing from one to the other a couple of times in one day!

You may also feel less motivated or excited about things that used to make you happy. This is also based on science, as the parts of your brain that stimulate excitement and passion also take a holiday during your teens. It can leave you more stressed than your younger siblings or the grown-ups.

Finally, there's part of the brain called the amygdala, which causes that 'FIGHT or FLIGHT' reaction to stress or fear. During your teens it's in overdrive, which is why you might be emotional, sensitive, angry or stressed. This, combined with the fact that you are not yet a ninja of communication, can be why you have so many arguments or misunderstandings with your friends or family.

So the next time you have a meltdown, take it easy on yourself. You can't be blamed for science!

YOUR BODY

THERE'S SO MUCH TO TALK ABOUT
WHEN IT COMES TO YOUR BODY,
HOW IT SERVES YOU, HOW YOU THINK
ABOUT IT, AND HOW YOU CARE FOR
AND NOURISH IT. LET'S DIVE IN ...

Your body is really amazing. Think about it; your body is a wonderful tool that carries your heart and soul through the world, allowing you to do so many things.

Every cell of your body is working for you; from your little toenail to the tip of your smallest eyelash. Each part works in unison to get you through each day, and most of the time you don't even need to tell it what to do! Your body changes so much over the teenage years it's hard to keep up. Before you know it, you've become a woman, one of the most amazing and most powerful creatures on earth.

TV, magazines, social media and advertising have been conning women for years into feeling insecure about our bodies. They try to convince us that our value is based on how we look, but we're not taking that any more! We need to recognise, reject and resist harmful messages about our bodies and what 'beauty' means.

Our bodies are not ornaments to be admired; they are the tools that allow us to make our mark on the world, to sing, dance, run, stretch, smile and hug.

Be kind to your body, and thank it for doing its best by taking care of it.

HOW TO BE MORE BODY-POSITIVE

+ **REMIND YOURSELF OF EVERYTHING THAT YOUR BODY ENABLES YOU TO DO** – Remember that your body is more than just an arrangement of skin, bones and muscles. It's a beautiful machine that will carry you to wherever your life takes you.

+ **THINK CRITICALLY ABOUT WHAT YOU SEE IN THE MEDIA** – The beauty industry wants you to believe that to be lovable, you have to cover yourself with 367 different types of creams, serums and lotions. They make billions from it. Someone smart once said, 'In a society that profits from your self-doubt, loving yourself is a rebellious act.' Be a rebel.

+ **ALL THE ACCOUNTS YOU FOLLOW ON INSTAGRAM THAT MAKE YOU FEEL BAD? UNFOLLOW** – Please get rid of them. Try to follow smart and strong people who empower and inspire you to be your best self. And always remember, your best self is allowed to eat cake.

+ **ACCEPT COMPLIMENTS** – When someone tells you you look amazing, or that they like your eyes, or that you have a lovely smile, don't rush to push the compliment away. Just enjoy the moment and say, 'Thank you'.

+ **HATERS ARE GONNA HATE** – Those Instagram accounts you unfollowed above? Now do the real-life version. The 'friend' who told you you'd be asked on more dates if you lost just a few pounds? Or the boyfriend who thinks you 'used to be fit'? They were right; you would definitely be better if you cut some weight – that dead weight you've been hanging out with for far too long. Cut them loose and set yourself free.

+ STOP COMPARING YOURSELF TO OTHERS – The girl in your class with gorgeous silky hair? We bet she wishes she had legs half as long as yours. Shake what your mama gave you!

+ BE KINDER TO YOUR BODY – Do us a favour and put your hand on your heart. (Go on, do it!) Can you feel your heart beating? That very same heart has beaten every second of every day, ever since your little baba eyes first opened. It beats when you are crying, when you are asleep, when you laugh, when you dance. Be kind to that heart; it protects you, and you've got to protect it right back too. Be your own best friend.

HOW DO WE LEARN ABOUT SEX?

Let's just be honest. Lots of us still have some questions about sex. Even saying the word brings some of us out in a hot flush of embarrassment – you might even spell it (S-E-X!) for fear of being struck down by either lightning or the ghost of Great-Aunt Brigid.

We learn most of what we know about sex in three ways:

+ The sex-ed talk we got at the end of primary school by the woman who looked like she worked in the library, who talked about straight man–woman intercourse in a clinical and emotionless way that wouldn't inspire anyone.

+ From your parents, who don't really want anyone to touch their little girl until you are at least 30; or if you could just become a nun, even better. Despite this, being able to have open conversations with parents where possible is great, if you can get over the initial cringiness.

+ From porn, which features hairless, well-lit, greased-up bodies, who always seem to be enjoying themselves immensely and are never awkward or funny.

Because we struggle to get honest, real advice that covers both the physical and emotional side of sex, we can end up with a pretty messed-up relationship with our sexuality, based on a mix of embarrassment, guilt and curiosity. We should be encouraged to know what we want, what works for us, and what we're comfortable with. We need better access in schools to sex-ed that is realistic and inclusive. It needs to be shame-free, empowering, and inclusive of the entire LGBT community.

IS PORN REAL?

The short answer to this is no. But far too many young people learn all they know about sex from porn. There's no shame in watching porn if you're curious and of an appropriate age, but here's what you need to know first ...

PORN ISN'T REALISTIC

Porn is a form of entertainment based on fantasy. It's heavily produced and choreographed to suit a formula created by the industry to get more views. The videos are mostly 5–10 minutes long, which doesn't leave the stars much time to eat a takeaway, complain that they feel bloated, watch an episode of *CSI* or put the bins out. Real-life relationships involve more awkwardness, bumbling, teeth bumping, and they should always start with a conversation about consent (more on that in Section 1).

Also, most bodies aren't quite as smooth as a dolphin, and might even have more butt pimples.

IT'S NOT USUALLY SAFE

Porn actors rarely use condoms, which doesn't promote safe sex as much as they maybe should. The truth is that using condoms doesn't spoil the experience or make it uncomfortable. The professional porn industry does have to do regular testing for STIs, but for the rest of us, we're better safe than sorry.

IT'S ADDICTIVE

Watching porn can release the same hit of dopamine that other addictions provide. The fact that porn is free makes it easy to access, and therefore become dependent on. If you think you might be developing a habit, you can do a quick test on www.virtual-addiction.com.

Always use reliable, shame-free, honest resources when it comes to answering any questions you might have about sex. Some people watch porn, and some don't. The most important thing to know is that in real life, be guided by what you enjoy and what makes you comfortable, in your own time, and at your own pace.

YOUR MENSTRUAL CYCLE: SO MUCH MORE THAN JUST YOUR PERIOD

We often think of our menstrual cycle in very simple terms – we're either on our period, or we're not. In reality, we go through a lot of changes even during our off-period days.

This piece was contributed by Orna Murray, one of the Shona Ambassadors! Orna has a wealth of knowledge when it comes to periods and performance; she has a degree in psychology and a master's in health psychology. She has worked with elite female athletes to help them understand how their minds and bodies can work together. So we asked her to talk us through the monthly cycle and how it's normal to feel different each and every morning.

Here's what you need to know:

The menstrual cycle is made up of four different phases, but most girls (and women!) don't think about their cycle other than when they are on their period. Your menstrual cycle is unique to you and it's a really important part of your health.

Periods are often seen as an inconvenience (or a curse), but despite what we are taught, we are designed to have healthy, pain-free periods. Although it is very common for girls to experience premenstrual syndrome (PMS) symptoms such as bloating, mood swings or fatigue in the few days coming up to their period, these symptoms are not something you just have to put up with – they are indicators that something is slightly out of balance.

Our menstrual cycles normally last anywhere between 21 and 35 days; however, this is just the average – it's normal to have shorter or longer cycles, especially when you are a teenager. Your body is constantly moving through a cycle, and knowing what is happening and why it's happening can change how you experience your cycle!

Your menstrual cycle has four phases:

PHASE 1
WINTER (DAYS 1–6 APPROX.)

Day one of your period marks the first day of your new menstrual cycle and the end of your last cycle. You might feel a dip in energy and maybe feel a little less sociable and crave some more alone time.

This is an important time to get to know yourself. If you're into art, writing, or long walks with your dog, now is the perfect time to do all those things. It's also a time to be really kind to your body and cosy up with hot water bottles, Netflix and warm drinks.

PHASE 2
SPRING (DAYS 7–13 APPROX.)

You'll naturally feel your energy start to increase and you'll begin to 'like' other people again. A great time to make lists, plan, and spring clean your room! It's normal to have days when you feel a bit frazzled – because your hormones are steadily rising – but this should even out in a few days. Get creative! Now is a brilliant time to try something new or start a project or challenge.

PHASE 3
SUMMER (DAYS 14–21 APPROX.)

Phase 3 is definitely the most fun and energetic part of your cycle. You might find it easier to get out of bed in the morning and you might feel very motivated. Your confidence tends to be higher during this time and a lot of girls feel that they are really themselves during this phase – happy, bubbly and confident. You might want to see your friends more, do more things in the evening and get projects done. It's an excellent time to be productive. Just like the summer itself, you feel enthusiastic and sunny on the inside.

PHASE 4
AUTUMN (DAYS 22–28 APPROX.)

You might notice a shift in how you feel. Your energy, although still high, is likely to be a little softer and more subtle. Phase 4 can be a really productive time as girls many girls find they can really focus on schoolwork, etc.

Towards the end of this phase you might start to notice some PMS – it's important to track any symptoms so that you can see any patterns and know what to expect. It is really important to get to bed early and eat your fruit and vegetables during this phase, as it should make your period more manageable.

Don't worry if this is all very new to you!

Start small by tracking your period. Log when you get your period and how you feel and how you felt the few days beforehand. You can track your period in a diary or there are lots of apps available now that help you track your menstrual cycle, e.g. FitrWoman, Clue, Flo and Period Tracker.

No matter what phase of your menstrual cycle you are in, you are still yourself. When you get to know your cycle, it is much easier to manage symptoms and be kinder to yourself.

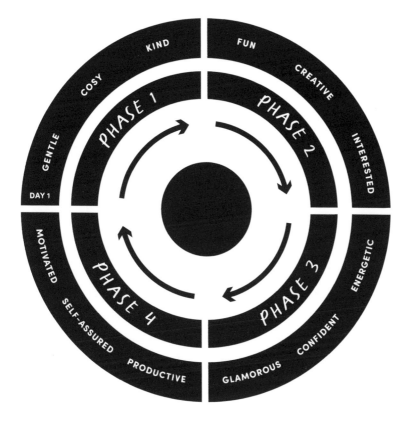

OUR TOP PERIOD HACKS

Everyone's experiences with periods are unique, and they change over time. It's not fun for anyone, and if you struggle with pain or heavy flow, it can have a massive effect on your daily life. The key to having a wonderful (?!?) period is to be prepared, and to give your body what it needs. (Note: If your periods are especially painful, have a chat with your doctor – there are things you can do to manage it.)

Here are our favourite period hacks:

+ **ALWAYS HAVE AN EMERGENCY KIT** – As the cub scouts say, you should always be prepared for an emergency, especially a period emergency. Try to keep a little zipped pouch at the bottom of your school bag, kit bag or handbag. Better safe than sorry. Have some spares for your less-organised friends too! Your kit should contain your weapon of choice (pads, tampons, pantyliners or menstrual cup), some spare knickers, a couple of paracetamol and a fiver. (The fiver is to buy yourself seven Mars bars for your lunch if you need to.)

+ **USE A PERIOD TRACKER** – There are loads of period trackers out there, and if your cycle is somewhat regular, it will give you all the warning you need so you don't get caught out. And you can make plans around it, like camping with your friends or having a swim-day. You can use an app, of which there are plenty, or a good old-fashioned calendar.

+ **HEAT** – Heat is great for period pain. A hot water bottle or a heat patch on your stomach can encourage blood circulation, giving you some relief. In an emergency, you can fill a sock with rice and heat it in the microwave. Genius!

+ **CAFFEINE** – Not many people know this, but coffee can cause your body to retain water, which makes your cramps and bloating worse. Salty foods are also a no-no, as they dehydrate you. Drink loads of water, which will flush your system out and give you more energy.

+ **BLOODSTAINS – Got some blood on your favourite jeans? No problem. The key is to get them in COLD water as soon as possible. If it's a particularly stubborn stain, try salt, lemon juice, or a paste made from baking soda or aspirin.**

+ **DIET AND SUPPLEMENTS – Broccoli, kale and spinach all contain iron, which can be depleted during heavy bleeds. You could also take supplements like evening primrose oil (for PMS), ginger (for bloating), fennel (for nausea or weakness), chasteberry and ginkgo leaf (for cramps). Always do your research on any supplements before you take them to learn about risks and side effects.**

Also, masturbation can act as a natural pain-reliever to help cramps, headaches, and back-pain. So, feel free to schedule some alone time.

TEN GENUINELY INTERESTING FACTS ABOUT PERIODS

Periods: your monthly reminder from Mother Nature that your body is a miracle of engineering, and that you are a superhuman who can do just about anything. Weird as periods are, hold on to your knickers, friends, because things are about to get a LOT weirder.

1 **YOU CAN GET YOUR PERIOD IN YOUR ACTUAL NOSE – Don't freak out; it's highly unlikely and very rare, but it's called 'vicarious menstruation', which means bleeding from somewhere other than your uterus. Women have bled from their eyes, noses**

and even lungs during their period. It occurs because the blood capillaries all over your body soften during menstruation, and sometimes allow blood to come out. Bloody deadly, eh?

2 **PERIODS HURT MORE WHEN IT'S COLD OUT** – Cold weather can also make your period last longer and be heavier. One more reason to move to Florida – who's in?

3 **PERIODS CAN MAKE YOU MORE STUPIDER** – Researchers at the University of Bath have found that our cognitive abilities dip slightly when Aunt Flo comes a-knocking. Tell this to your teachers when they give you grief for not being your usual sparky self for the next test, and get them to reschedule the Junior and Leaving Cert if it clashes with your fun times.

4 **HUMANS, HUMPBACK WHALES AND ELEPHANTS ARE THE ONLY ANIMALS THAT GO THROUGH MENOPAUSE** – So don't mess with the big ladies. (Whales and elephants, we mean. Not you, Grandma.)

5 **YOU DON'T BLEED AS MUCH AS YOU THINK YOU DO.** It can get messy, but it's only about six teaspoons over the 3–7 days; the rest is other even grosser stuff. (Sorry.)

6 **IF YOU HAVE LONG CYCLES, IT'S BECAUSE YOUR EGGS ARE LAZY** – After you ovulate, some eggs race down the fallopian tubes to the uterus and others stop off at the Obama Plaza for coffee and take lots of naps.

7 **CLOTS ARE MADE BY CONTRACTIONS** – Yep, as in labour contractions. Like teeny-tiny mini ones. (The real ones are a

LOT worse – ask your ma.) In fact, most period symptoms, like cramping, nausea, bloating, moodiness, appetite and sore boobs, feel pretty close to early pregnancy.

8 IN THE MIDDLE AGES, PEOPLE THOUGHT RED-HAIRED PEOPLE WERE CONCEIVED DURING A PERIOD – But in fairness, they thought lots of stupid stuff, so let's go easy on them. Now we have SCIENCE!

9 THE URGE TO SHOP BEFORE YOUR PERIOD IS LEGIT – A study at the University of Hertfordshire found that women are more likely to go on a shopping spree ten days before their period than any other time of the month. So if payday falls at the same time, hide your wallet from yourself.

10 MENSTRUAL BLOOD USED TO CURE EVERYTHING – Well, no, it didn't, but people thought it did. In ye olden times, it was used as a medicine for everything from leprosy to headaches to warts to DEMONIC POSSESSION. Personally, we'd rather take a paracetamol and soldier on, thanks all the same.

And finally, a bonus fact …

11 DISNEY MADE A MOVIE ABOUT PERIODS – Made in 1946, the movie is called *The Story of Menstruation*. It's not great, TBH – no singing, no dancing snowmen. We recommend you give it a miss. But it is the first time the word 'vagina' was used in a movie, so that's lovely, so it is.

WHAT IS THRUSH (NOT THE BIRD, THE OTHER ONE)?

Most women and girls will suffer from thrush at some stage and it usually starts with a rather awkward itch. Dr Sharon O'Donnell is our go-to GP whenever we have questions about our bodies. Here she explains thrush to us in detail.

WHAT'S THRUSH ANYWAY?

Thrush, or *Candida* infection, is a common yeast infection that can affect women and men.

WHAT CAUSES IT?

There is a natural balance between the good bacteria and harmful bacteria in our bodies. Certain factors can influence this balance and cause the bad bacteria and yeast to exceed the normal good bacteria, which can result in a range of symptoms.

Vaginal thrush is the most common infection, with symptoms of thick white cottage cheese-like vaginal discharge as well as vulval and vaginal redness and itch and some stinging when passing urine.

Oral thrush can also occur, causing a sore mouth and white coating on the tongue and gums. Antibiotic treatments, being run-down and having diabetes or a high-sugar diet are common causes of thrush.

HOW IS IT DIAGNOSED?

It is often diagnosed based on symptoms alone, but your doctor may do a vaginal swab to confirm the diagnosis, particularly if it's not your first time getting symptoms. Home test kits are also available in pharmacies. With vaginal symptoms, it is also important to exclude other possible causes of the symptoms, like sexually transmitted infections. While *Candida* or thrush can be spread by sexual contact, it is not classified as a sexually transmitted disease as such.

WHAT IS THE TREATMENT?

Usually, treatment is easy, and involves cream to ease the itch and vaginal pessaries (tablets that are inserted into the vagina). Canesten is the usual brand used. There are also oral tablets that can be taken as a once-off (Diflucan). It is important if sexual activity has taken place that the partner of the affected person is also treated.

There is mixed evidence as to the benefit of trying to re-boost our body's own natural bacteria with probiotic supplements.

WHAT IF I KEEP GETTING SYMPTOMS?

It is important to see your doctor, who may advise a longer course of treatment after excluding other causes of your symptoms such as STIs or urinary tract infections and may suggest doing blood tests to rule out diabetes. A change in your diet to a low-sugar, low-yeast diet excluding highly processed sugary foods and pizza dough, bread, mushrooms, grapes and alcohol may also help – this is the '*Candida* diet'.

OTHER GYNAECOLOGICAL ISSUES IN TEENS

Here are a few other potential gynaecological issues you should know about.

+ **TOXIC SHOCK SYNDROME** – This is very rare. It is an overwhelming infection of your body with staphylococcal or sometimes streptococcal bacteria that release toxic substances that can cause severe, potentially fatal, illness. A number of things can cause it. It is most notoriously and commonly caused by the use of tampons for too long or forgotten tampons. Leaving a tampon in for more than eight hours is therefore not recommended.

+ **ENDOMETRIOSIS** – In endometriosis, tissue that looks and acts like the lining of the uterus starts growing in places surrounding the uterine cavity. It can result in severe pain in the pelvis, heavy periods and lower back pain.

+ **OVARIAN CYSTS** – These are fluid-filled sacs or pockets in an ovary or on its surface. They can be quite common in our teens, and most just require observation or some medication. Sometimes, if the cysts grow large, they may require surgery. Symptoms include pelvic pain (a sharp or dull ache on one side of your tummy), or a bloated or full-feeling tummy.

If things don't feel right down south, it could be for any number of reasons and most are easily fixed after a quick visit to your doctor. Don't ever be worried about making an appointment; doctors see all sorts every day. If it makes you feel more comfortable, ask to see a female GP.

You'll notice that a lot of conditions have similar symptoms, so really the only way to diagnose your issue is to see a doctor. And remember, Google is not a doctor!

FIVE WAYS TO LOVE YOUR BODY

How many Instagram memes do we see every day telling us to be more body positive? To embrace our curves. Loving the skin we're in is easier said than done, especially when we're bombarded all day long with images of women who don't look like us. Those ideals are deeply ingrained in our subconscious, and changing how we feel about them is a long, tough process. But it's worth working on. Here are five tips that might help:

1 **TUNE INTO YOUR SOCIAL MEDIA FEEDS – They have more of an impact on how you feel about yourself than you would think. Make sure that your feed is balanced and features all sorts of people with different shapes, sizes, ages and colours. When you take a selfie, how many shots, angles and filters do you try before you're happy to post? Remember that celebrities and**

influencers do this too! They squeeze their spots and hold in their tummies, just like the rest of us do.

2   **BEING HEALTHY DOESN'T INVOLVE GIVING UP ALL THE THINGS THAT MAKE YOU HAPPY** – Why not focus on adding things to your life, like more water, more movement, or more sleep? Don't cut out foods that you love, or do types of exercise that you hate. Create your own way and stop punishing yourself. Find what you love and do more of that!

3   **TALK NICELY TO YOURSELF** – Stop being critical. No matter what shape or size you are, you deserve love and kindness, especially from yourself. This takes practice, but being more aware of it is a good start.

4   **STOP COMPARING YOURSELF TO OTHERS** – They are not you, and you are not them. And they have their own hang-ups and insecurities to worry about. The only person you should be competing with is 'yesterday you'. Some days you'll win, and some days she'll have you beat.

5   **SET YOURSELF AN ACTIVITY-BASED GOAL** – Like a couch-to-5k or a yoga class. Focus on the progress you make, and you will start to feel better about yourself and appreciate your body for the beautiful thing she is. Focus on how much stronger, faster or more flexible you feel. Feed your body to fuel that energy, not to punish her for not living up to your expectations.

Give a girl a break!

Learning to love your body will take as long as learning to dislike it did. Why not consciously, every day, consider all the amazing things your body has done for you today, and whisper a little 'thank you' as you put yourself to bed?

HEY! GO TO BED!

Everyone loves their bed. It's our happy place.

Sleep is the single most positive thing we can do for ourselves, mentally, emotionally and physically. On the other hand, not getting enough sleep has a negative effect on your mood, weight, hormone levels, concentration and general ability to deal with the daily drama.

Lots of us struggle to sleep, spending hour after hour looking at the ceiling and bargaining with ourselves to go asleep now, okay now, okay definitely now, until we see the sunrise and hear the birds starting a new day.

Here are some sure-fire ways to get those extra Zs:

+ **TAKE A NAP** – Did you know that 85 per cent of mammals take short naps throughout the day? And did you know that in lots of cultures, afternoon power-naps or siestas are a thing? If you find yourself slumping in the afternoon, a quick forty winks might leave you refreshed. This might be tricky in school, but a quick one when you get home might do. Twenty minutes is the perfect nap time – any longer and you will wake up groggier. Find a quiet spot, set your alarm and curl up like a cat. Enjoy.

+ **EXERCISE** – Getting enough exercise has loads of benefits when it comes to sleep. It can stop you feeling sleepy during the day but leave you just ready to sleep by bedtime. It can also improve the quality of your sleep; in fact, some doctors recommend it as a cure for insomnia. Make sure you leave enough time before bed for your body to unwind or you'll be too pumped to nod off.

+ **PAIN** – If you are in pain, it can cause sleep deprivation. Apart from chronic pain, tight or sore muscles, or even jumpy legs, can leave you in a vicious cycle of not sleeping, and then stressing about not sleeping. A massage or a hot bath can help relax your entire body and get you in the sleep zone.

+ **LIGHT** – Before gas or electric lighting were invented, people just went to bed when it got dark. Sure, what else was there to do? Now, our sleeping patterns are all skewed, and our bodies can't keep up. Too much bright light can keep your body in full-steam-ahead mode, which pushes you to stay up later. Listen, not to sound like your ma, but keep your screen-time to a minimum before bed, and leave your devices outside your bedroom when it's time to go to sleep. Turn your alarm clock towards the wall, and shut those curtains as tight as possible. It would help if you created a ritual at night to tell your body to start moving from commotion to calm. You can't go from full-on mayhem to face-down snoring in ten minutes. Dial down the energy at least an hour before bedtime, turn down the lights, and keep yourself cosy.

+ If you're still struggling to sleep, here's the quick-fire round:
  - Avoid stressful TV (stick with books or podcasts if you can).

- Try herbal tea – peppermint is good. Just steer clear of caffeine.

- Clear your mind by making a to-do list for tomorrow, or write in your journal.

- Try not to have long phone calls, FaceTimes or group chats close to bedtime.

- Stretch, meditate, or follow a yoga class on YouTube.

- Have a cute goodnight hug with someone who loves you.

MOVE YOUR BODY!

There are so many benefits to exercise, and there are so many ways to do it, so there should be an option available to everyone.

Choosing to move wherever or whenever you can is one of the best ways to stay healthy. Some of us like to compete – pushing ourselves to win, beating other teams or people, running marathons or jumping out of planes. Some of us like to express ourselves more artistically by dancing, drumming or doing yoga. Some of us hate exercise because we never enjoyed PE, or getting mucky or being in the great outdoors.

The benefits come from raising your heart rate, so whatever works for you works for your body as well. It makes you feel good too! Here's the science:

+ Exercise helps distract you from your worries by focusing on your own performance.

+ Exercise is a great way to meet other people and feel part of a community.

+ Exercise releases happy chemicals in your brain, such as serotonin and endorphins. All the good stuff!

+ Exercise helps you to sleep better.

Exercise doesn't mean you have to lift heavy barbells in the gym or run 20 miles before school. Simply trying to get 10,000 steps a day, eating well and getting enough activity is plenty in order for you to live your best life.

HOW TO NOURISH YOUR BODY

Lets be honest, there aren't many of us who haven't had a love/hate relationship with our bodies. As women, we're taught that the skinnier we become, the greater our worth. We feel guilty for eating cake and embarrassed asking for a second helping. Our relationships with food and our weight are built on shame. This needs to change.

As teenagers, our bodies need more nourishment than ever. We are going through huge physical, mental and emotional changes. In order to thrive, you need to nourish that gorgeous body, listen to what it needs and be in tune with how good food makes you feel.

Nutritionist Rebecca Garvey is here to tell us how we can eat better so that we perform better.

As a nutritionist, the one question I get asked lot by girls is 'What should I be eating?' To begin, the word 'should' should be banned (excuse the joke). When we use the word 'should' we straightaway make ourselves feel guilty and inadequate, like we're not measuring up to everyone else: 'I should be eating more vegetables', 'I should be drinking more water', 'I should be getting more hours' sleep.' Just reading that can make you feel bad.

Instead, we need to replace the word with 'could'. 'Could' allows us to replace a guilty statement with an opportunity. 'What could I be eating?' 'What could I be eating to give me more energy?' 'What could I be eating to help me concentrate better in school?' 'What could I be eating to help me feel good, to help me remain calm, to help me sleep better, to help me start the day on the right foot?' Because all these questions are some of the ways food can help us; we just sometimes don't realise it. Ask yourself the question, 'What do you use food for?' A bit of an odd question, and the answer most people will say is 'Eh, to feed me when I'm hungry.' Which, of course, is very true; but food can have a much greater meaning and function in our lives. By becoming a little bit more aware about the different functions of food and how it can work for us, we can actually start getting more out of our food than just filling a gap. Using food to not only fuel us but to help us in many aspects of our lives – concentration, focus, mood, anxiety, connecting and celebrating with friends and family.

Even though I have studied and worked with food for many years, I am still learning new things every single day, so I completely understand that food and nutrition can be extremely confusing, with a lot of conflicting opinions about what is good and bad for us. So, to help combat the confusion, here are six of the most important things about food and how best it can serve not just to fuel you but to support you through a busy and often stressful life.

ALWAYS EAT BREAKFAST

You've probably already heard this, but it is number one because the importance of a good breakfast for success throughout the entire school day cannot be overemphasised. When you wake up, your blood sugar is low, which means your energy is low. Guess what organ uses sugar the most? That's right – the brain. And what organ gets used the most when sitting in class? The brain. So, if you haven't fuelled your brain at the beginning of the day, concentration and focus in school are going to be really challenging. Teenage girls are more prone to skip breakfast than teenage boys, so, girls, let's get those brains alive and kicking first thing in the morning. Porridge, wholegrain or sourdough toast with a variety of toppings, such as peanut butter, scrambled eggs or chopped banana, and fruit salads with yoghurt and nuts are all fantastic options.

EAT THE RAINBOW

This means to try and have as much colour as possible in your meals. Lots of colour in your lunch: greens (lettuce, spinach, cucumber), reds and purples (tomatoes, chilli, cabbage, beetroot), yellow and orange (sweetcorn, peppers, carrots) as well as a piece of fruit. Why? Fruits and vegetables with rich vibrant colours contain something called phytonutrients. When we are working and studying really hard or find ourselves in stressful situations, we build up molecules in our bodies called free radicals. The phytonutrients help to mop up these free radicals and keep us healthy and immune to illnesses, such as flus, coughs and colds, which is really important, especially coming into winter.

ESSENTIAL FATS

The name kind of gives it away – these guys are essential to our health. Why? Your brain is 60 per cent fat! So we need the right kinds of fat to maintain a healthy brain for learning and memory. There are many types, but omega-3 fatty acid is the star pupil when it comes to the best type of essential fat. Omega-3 can be found in many foods. One of the best sources is fish. Okay, opening a can of tuna may not make you very popular at the canteen table, but having fish like smoked salmon, salmon fillet, mackerel or kippers will help with your Omega-3 intake. If fish isn't your thing, go for nuts or seeds, which are crammed full of essential fats. A handful of nuts, such as walnuts, almonds or Brazil nuts, is a great option for a snack. Or you could sprinkle some chia seeds on your breakfast in the morning. Choosing a snack with essential fats can also have the added benefit of reducing sugar cravings.

CHOOSE COMPLEX CARBOHYDRATES

Carbohydrates can be a little confusing: wholegrain, wholemeal, simple sugars and so on. The word 'complex' just means that the carbohydrate has fibre. The fibre is very thick and takes longer to break down in the body. This is good news for us for two reasons. First, it takes longer to break down and digest, which means it stays in our stomach for longer and makes us feel fuller so we don't get as hungry as quickly as we would if we were eating a non-complex carb such as white bread or white pasta. Second, the fibre causes the carb to be released slowly into the bloodstream. This means no sugar spikes. Sugar spikes have been shown to cause mood swings, reduce concentration and irritate the skin. Complex carbs include wholegrain bread, wholemeal pasta, oats and brown rice.

STAY HYDRATED

We've all heard that we should drink 6–8 glasses of water a day. But why is it important to be well hydrated? The brain sits in fluid, which is mainly made up of water. If we do not stay hydrated, this fluid reduces and our brain does not work as effectively. Ideally, always have a bottle of water with you throughout the day. Coming into winter, hot drinks, especially herbal teas, are an easy way to keep you warm and hydrated.

ENJOY

Food is meant to be enjoyed. Even your daily dinner is an opportunity to sit and socialise and catch up with friends and family. Enjoy your food, be thankful for it and be sure to have dessert now and again. It's a balance. All work and no play!

WHY WATER IS YOUR BEST FRIEND

On the previous page, Rebecca mentioned the importance of staying hydrated. Why does anyone need to be told to drink more water? It's obvious, right? Well, this may seem boring to you, but let's explore why it's so important.

+ **IT WAKES YOUR BRAIN UP** – If you struggle to concentrate in class, you might be a little dehydrated. Studies show that drinking water improves your mental function and cognitive ability. Oh, hey there, seven H1s in the Leaving Cert!

+ **IT HELPS YOUR PHYSICAL PERFORMANCE** – Drinking water helps your heart pump more strongly, which drives more oxygen to your muscles. It also keeps your body cool and your joints lubricated.

+ **IT MAKES YOUR SKIN GLOW** – The beauty industry doesn't want you to know this, as they make money from every face mask you buy, but the best way to get moisture to your skin is to drink it. It gives your skin that healthy glow and makes it plumper and brighter.

+ **IT HELPS DIGESTION** – If you sometimes get a little 'backed up', it could be because your system needs more liquid to flush it out. Dehydration can feel like hunger, which makes you eat more, which can back you up even more, and on it goes.

+ **IT'S FREE** – You guys, it's literally on tap!

+ **IT MAKES YOU FEEL AMAZING** – With all the regular pooping, the glowing skin and the straight As, how could you not feel on top of the world?

HOW TO TELL IF YOU NEED TO DRINK MORE WATER

First up, look at your pee! The lighter it is, the more hydrated you are. If it's quite yellow, you need to hit the tap. Other symptoms include a dry mouth, headaches, fatigue, sunken eyes, constipation, dry skin, joint pain and muscle cramps.

Set yourself a water goal every day (2 litres for an A* from us!), carry your water bottle everywhere, and get as much into you as possible.

WHAT'S THE DEAL WITH SPOTS?

We're back with our good pal Dr Sharon O'Donnell, and this time she is telling us about spots.

Spots are blocked pores which get infected with bacteria and make red raised lumps on our skin.

Around puberty – from age ten onwards – because of your changing hormones, your skin produces more oil or sebum, which blocks the pores. The bacteria in our skin love this! Species of bacteria such as *Propionibacterium acnes* [don't you just love that name?] grow and cause infection and lead to spots or pimples or zits – whatever you like to call them. Blocked pores alone are called blackheads or comedones, and infected ones are called whiteheads and if severe are painful pustules.

Acne affects most people at some stage in their lives, but it's most common during the teen years. Mainly the face is affected, but people can get spots all over their chest and back too.

Acne is NOT caused by poor hygiene or a bad diet! Some people survive on takeaways and fizzy drinks and never get a spot. There may be some foods, like chocolate, that cause flare-ups, so if they do don't eat them! If your parents had spots, you will probably get them too.

And obviously, a healthy diet helps in so many other ways, but that's a chat for another day.

TIPS FOR BETTER SKIN

+ Keep your skin clean. Remove make-up well every day.

+ Eat a healthy diet – for so many other reasons too.

+ Get lots of sleep to keep you looking healthy.

+ Drink lots of water.

+ Don't smoke – it ages your skin prematurely, greys your complexion and leads to earlier wrinkles.

+ Many over-the-counter products are available for treating spots, such as good old Sudocrem and Clearasil-type products.

+ There is no need to live with terrible spots any more so ask your GP for help or tell your friends, including boys with bad skin, who can often be even more self-conscious than the girls!

ARE YOU REALLY WHAT YOU WEAR?

Should we wear make-up or follow fashion trends? The answer seems pretty clear: girls and women should wear whatever the hell they want as long as it's on their own terms and makes them happy.

Some people consider make-up an art form; they enjoy the ritual of applying it and find it relaxing or therapeutic. For others, it gives them confidence, and that's fine too. Whether you're sporty, edgy, high-fashion or bohemian, your style is unique to you.

However, here are some handy fashion tips. They're not based on what you should wear above or below a certain age. They're also not based around flattering your size. And they're for sure not aimed at attracting other people.

+ **DRESS FOR YOU, AND NO ONE ELSE** – What influences your clothing choices? Do you buy things because you think others will like them even if you're not sure yourself? Are you a slave to what's currently in fashion? Do you wear high heels even though you hate walking in them? Don't be afraid to swim out of the mainstream when it comes to your own style.

+ **DISCOVER YOUR OWN STYLE** – If you're not sure what you're into in terms of your style, do some self-discovery. Look at the people who influence you and use them as inspiration, adapting their style to suit your own needs. Sometimes it takes time, but you'll get there eventually once you trust your own instincts.

+ **WEAR WHAT MAKES YOU FEEL GOOD** – Research shows that you often pick your clothes based on your mood. If you're feeling confident, it might be a red jacket and lots of jewellery day. If you need a down day, soft leggings and huggy hoodies might be better.

+ **DON'T BE A SLAVE TO FAST FASHION** – You might feel like you need to spend all your money on fast fashion sites to keep up with the cool kids. Or that you can never wear the same thing to a party twice. This is a bad habit to get into, and online shopping can be addictive. You really only need a few key pieces that you love to always look amazing. Use websites like Depop or spend your Saturdays in charity shops to find items that are unique and cheap!

+ **EXPRESS YOURSELF!** If you feel uncomfortable in what you wear, it shows in your body language. On the flip side, if you LOVE your outfit, you will strut into every room with serious swagger. It's your confidence that people find attractive; your outfit or make-up just add some extra glitter to an already fabulous presence.

Always remember – it is not your job to just show up and look pretty. Your appearance is just the icing on the cake, and not the whole cake. It's how it tastes that really matters. Leave a trail of glitter and gloriousness wherever you go, whatever that even means to you.

SECTION 4

YOUR WORLD

THE WORLD IS A BIG, BEAUTIFUL

PLACE, FULL OF MANY DIFFERENT

TYPES OF PEOPLE, FAMILIES,

TRIBES, COMMUNITIES AND

CULTURES.

While it's very important to look inside yourself and figure out who you are, it's just as important to look outside yourself and be aware of the world around you and figure out how you can use your talents, skills and interests to contribute to that world in a positive way.

The world needs people who think differently, who can help to solve the problems we are currently facing. Those problems can seem vast and overwhelming, and you shouldn't believe for a minute that you're responsible for solving them all. There are so many ways in which you can use the parts of yourself that are considered 'different' in a positive and powerful way.

When you find your passion, do what you can, when you can, and together we can all make the world a better place.

WHERE DO I START?

Over the past few years, there has been a massive uprising by the young people of Ireland. Gone are the days when young people should be seen and not heard. Irish teens care about the world that they will inherit and want to do what they can to make it better.

What do you care about? Climate change? Equality? Diversity? Politics? Human rights? Homelessness? Feminism? Youth representation? Education? Pick one issue, and get stuck in.

Here's where you can start.

+ ASK QUESTIONS – There's more to education than what you learn in school. Learn as much as you can about the world by asking loads of questions. Our favourite question is 'Why?' Why do people behave as they do? Why do we do things this way? Why do we make assumptions about those who are 'different' from us? Why do we still use so much plastic?

+ UNDERSTAND – We all enjoy lovely chats with people who feel exactly the same as we do about everything. But this causes division among us. Have a rational and grown-up conversation with people who see the world differently from you. Try to understand their points of view and challenge your own.

+ TAKE ACTION – Start somewhere. Anywhere. The world's problems are too big for any one person to solve. But if everyone makes a little contribution it can be transformative. You can start small by getting involved in a litter pick, volunteering at an animal shelter, making choices about sustainable fashion or writing letters to the people who make decisions that affect you.

HOW TO BE AN ACTIVIST

Sophie is here to tell us her top tips for becoming more active in our communities and speaking up against injustice.

It's so important for us to use our voices and stand up for what we believe in. Don't for one minute feel that because you are young, or because you are a girl, no one will listen. It doesn't matter whether it's animal welfare, environmental issues, women's rights or your right to wear pants instead of a kilt in school. Formulate a solid argument, stand up, speak loudly and work as a team. Big things can happen.

We are often told by people who don't 'get' feminism that we should give up the fight and be happy with what we have. My response: as women, we are where we are today because of feminism and activism. We are a little more equal, a little louder and well on our way to true equality. And just like all the amazing, strong women before us, we are not content just because we can vote – and neither should we be. Believing in something, being passionate about some sort of injustice and standing up against it, is an incredible thing. Stand up and be counted for what you believe in.

Activism is all about getting engaged with issues you care about, stuff that makes you angry and makes you want to change the world. It is important to communicate and engage with what you want for yourself and your future self, and for others. You don't have to be an expert on the issue. What you do have to have is belief. Know that courage and activism are what got you the right to education, the right to vote, the right to have both a career and a family. There are still many more things to achieve.

What not to do is put on your blinkers and narrow your mind. Unfortunately, many people who feel strongly about specific issues don't take others' opinions into account. We are all guilty of this at times, but try not to fall into this trap, even if it seems like the most comfortable option. We have a lot to gain and learn from people who think differently from us. Understanding why they feel a certain way on an issue you are passionate about makes you better able to stand up for yourself.

Unfortunately, getting the courage to speak out is sometimes difficult for girls; our insecurities and personal hang-ups can hold us back. It's hard to love yourself all the time, and everyone struggles with this, but we can't let it stop us going out and demanding better. There are days I want to stay under the covers. On these days, I still try to read or write an article on something I care about.

Activism is about being a part of a bigger picture, a bigger goal, and helping to achieve this is a great way to get to know people and to know yourself better. Whether it's women's rights, LGBTQI rights, animal rights, go and agitate and be a part of the campaign. If you're passionate about women in sports or science, or if it's politics that excites you, express this in whatever way you can.

HOW TO BE AN ALLY

Have you ever heard the term 'Check your privilege'?

It simply means that while we all have challenges in our lives, some of us have certain advantages over others. This doesn't make any of us better than anyone else; it just means that society values some identities over others. We know this is wrong, and we're working on it as a human race, but we need to keep it in mind when it comes to other people. This applies not just to sexuality and gender identity but also to ethnicity, class and mental health.

By pure luck, you might have been born a few steps higher on the social ladder than others. It doesn't make you a bad person, but it does give you a responsibility to use your privilege to help and support others, so that every one of us has a fighting chance to succeed.

Being an ally means using your privilege to help stand up for those who need support. Here are some ways you can help:

+ **LISTEN** – This is the most important thing you can do. Never assume that you understand someone's experience without hearing their story. Listening is not always easy. Sometimes you will hear stories and realise that you might have been guilty of oppression in the past. Don't get hung up on feeling guilty; use it as an opportunity to learn and do better in future. Trust and believe what people tell you, give them space to speak, and respectfully ask questions. Just because you can't see the problem in your own life does not mean that it doesn't exist.

+ LEARN – It is not the responsibility of those who have been oppressed to teach you everything you need to know. It's your responsibility to invest your time in learning as much as you can. There are loads of resources out there, including documentaries, movies, books, podcasts and YouTube clips. Watch out for fake news and only use reliable sources. As a society, our prejudices are deeply ingrained over generations. We have to unlearn the harmful stuff so we can do better. This means taking a look at our own behaviour and that of our families, our governments and our leaders.

+ SPEAK UP – This is the hard bit. When you are experiencing discrimination, defending yourself can be scary and dangerous. Those of us with social power can't stand silently by. It takes a strong person to stand up for themselves, but an even stronger person to speak up for others. There are small ways we can all do this. If you hear someone make a cruel joke, don't laugh. If you feel comfortable doing so, say, 'That's not okay!' or 'I don't think it's cool to say things like that.'

+ SHOW UP – If your friend invites you to go with them to an event, watch a documentary, celebrate Pride, attend a march or protest, go with them and offer support. The issues might not affect you directly, but if they are important to your friends make it your business to get involved. Also, make sure that you include as many people as you can in your friend group and always extend an invite to someone who might appreciate it more than you think.

+ **DON'T MAKE ASSUMPTIONS** – Just because someone hasn't come out or doesn't look a certain way doesn't mean you know their story. Someone close to you might be trying to pluck up the courage to come out. Make sure everyone knows that you are accepting and supportive of them no matter what.

+ **WATCH YOUR LANGUAGE** – Using a person's correct pronoun can be transformative for them, as it decreases their risk of depression and other mental health issues. It's not up to you to choose their pronouns. Be led by them and respect their wishes. It's a small thing, but it shows respect.

+ The important thing to remember is that until we all are treated equally, we all need to work hard to create that fairer world for everyone.

TEN WAYS YOU CAN SAVE THE PLANET

It's all looking a bit grim at the moment. The rainforests are burning, the weather has gone crazy and it's all very worrying. As if you didn't have enough to worry about already, we can add eco-anxiety to the list. One of the things that contributes to this anxiety is the feeling of helplessness. The only cure is action. Once we all educate ourselves and do our bit, we can regain a little bit of control over our futures. How? Well, here are some ideas:

1 STAY INFORMED – Sign up to newsletters from organisations like Greenpeace, watch documentaries or hit up YouTube. (Watch out for fake news!)

2 REDUCE, REUSE, RECYCLE – Set your family the challenge of reducing your plastic use by 20–30 per cent. There are so many ways to do this, even down to your menstrual products!

3 START A COMPOST HEAP (OR A COMPOST BIN) – Throw all your organic waste in a pile at the bottom of the garden and let nature do its thing.

4 THINK ABOUT THE CLOTHES YOU BUY – Research ethical and eco-friendly brands. And please, in case it doesn't go without saying, stay away from fur!

5 HIT UP YOUR CHARITY SHOP – Trust us, there is nothing more rewarding than finding treasures in your local charity shop. Even better, why not hold a clothes-swap party with your friends? It's a great way to meet up and refresh your wardrobe at the same time. And it helps you save money too!

6 AVOID THE DRYER – Tumble dryers use so much energy, and they shrink your favourite jumpers. Get a clothes horse.

7 GROW YOUR VEG – It's amazing how much of your veg is flown or shipped from the other side of the world. What a waste of energy! Get yourself a window box and stick some tomatoes, garlic, lettuce or carrots in there.

8 CHECK YOUR PRODUCTS – Learn as much as you can about the

chemicals in your deodorants, cosmetics or hair dyes. Also, you can buy shampoo bars and save on plastic bottles.

9 **TRY TO AVOID ONE-WEAR OUTFITS** – What a waste of money. Make sure each loved item of clothing gets to live a full and happy life by styling it up, customising it, or lending it to friends (the ones who will care for it).

10 **CUT BACK YOUR MEAT INTAKE** – Much of the damage is being caused by methane, a.k.a. cow farts. It's okay to love your burgers, but if we all have one meat-free day per week, we will reduce methane gases by a seventh, which is a start.

So there you have it! Lots of ways we can all contribute and do our bit. Let's keep this beautiful planet around for as long as possible.

YOUR STARTER GUIDE TO REUSABLE PERIOD PRODUCTS

You learned loads of handy hacks for your period on page 140. But did you know that you can have an eco-friendly period too? If you've been thinking about trying reusable period products for a while, read on, sister!

Over your entire life, you will have your period for about six and a half years in total. Over that time you will use 11,000 disposable products and spend about €132 per year, which is a lot of money better spent on other essentials like cookie dough ice cream and keyrings with sloths on them. We also need to consider the environment, and especially the fact that 28,000 tampons and applicators wash up on beaches all over the world every day!

So what are your options?

+ **REUSABLE PADS** – These are pads that are made out of fabric. They're used in the same way as disposable pads, expect that you wash them after use. You can bring a zip bag to school to keep used pads in until you get home. Reusable pads can last for years.

+ **PERIOD UNDERWEAR** – These pants have unique in-built layers to soak up the blood. They are expensive to buy – at about €30 a pop – but they last for years. Period pants are very comfortable and are great for sport and other physical activities.

+ **PERIOD CUPS** – A cup might look uncomfortable, but honestly, when fitted properly, you won't even know it's there. Its sits inside your vagina, and you just empty it into the loo when you need to. This is an excellent investment at about €25, and it will last you for years – unless the dog gets hold of it!

You can find loads more information on all of this stuff on YouTube, or ask your doctor next time you're in for a check-up.

WHAT IS PERIOD POVERTY?

Periods are a normal bodily function, experienced by about half the world's female population every month. Yet we still struggle to talk openly about how they affect our lives.

Period products, like pads and tampons, can be expensive and can put women under serious financial pressure. 'Period poverty' refers to the lack of access to what we consider to be the essentials, like sanitary products, period education or even proper bathrooms.

Plan International, a fantastic organisation that advocates for girls worldwide, tells us that almost half of teenage girls in Ireland struggle to afford pads and tampons, even though they are not taxed here. In fact, many girls miss school every month because of it.

Hopefully, in the future, every school will have a bank of sanitary products that are readily available to anyone who needs them. This is something that you can start yourself, or you can get a group together and start a petition. You could start a pad or tampon donation box, where those who can afford them drop them in for use by those who can't.

We girls have so much to do, what with smashing glass ceilings, breaking boundaries, and kicking ass. No one should be left behind because they have a uterus.

To learn more about period poverty, here in Ireland and worldwide, check out www.plan.ie.

WHY REPRESENTATION MATTERS

Media is a small word that has a massive impact on us. It includes TV, movies, radio, newspapers and magazines, as well as our old friend social media. The media plays a powerful role in shaping your ideas and opinions about the world around you, and it provides a very narrow view of what it means to be a girl in Ireland today. This is why we need more **REPRESENTATION**.

For example, if you do a Google search for the word 'worker', your screen will fill with images of white men in hard hats. You won't see a variety of women and men of different ages, shapes, sizes or ethnicities working in a variety of jobs from scientists to make-up artists to astronauts to athletes to actors to parents who work at home caring for their families.

There is no single definition of what a woman should look like. Our media needs to work harder to make sure that each and every one of us feels represented, no matter what we look like from the outside or how we feel on the inside.

Always ask questions about the messages you see and look out for the amazing women who are doing amazing things and changing the world. They are there, and they're getting **LOUDER**!

TWENTY INTERESTING FACTS ABOUT WOMEN

Women are deadly. We know this. But here are some interesting facts about the fairer sex that you may not have heard before:

1   The two highest IQ scores ever recorded belonged to women.

2   In 1650 it was proposed in the British parliament that any women who wore make-up should be prosecuted for witchcraft.

3   More women than men graduate with third-level degrees in Ireland (52.5% vs 47.5%).

4   In the 1940s, advertising for women promoted weight gain, as curvy women were considered more attractive.

5   *Wonder Woman* (2017) was the first-ever superhero movie to be directed by a woman and have a female lead.

6   Every 90 seconds, a woman in the world dies from complications during childbirth.

7   In Albania, some women live as men to avoid restrictions placed on them by society. They change their hair, clothes, mannerisms and even names to be more masculine, and they also take an oath of celibacy.

8   Fancy ladies in the nineteenth century would never use the word 'leg' as it was too provocative. They would say 'limb' instead.

9   Widow-burning (Sati) used to be a common occurrence in India

and Nepal. To show their love for their dead husbands, women would burn themselves alive. Although it was supposed to be voluntary, many were drugged or pushed into the fire.

10 A 42-year-old female schoolteacher was the first person to ever ride down Niagara Falls in a barrel and survive.

11 Women started to wear high heels to copy men, who wore them in the 1600s to appear more manly.

12 When you take paid and unpaid work (housework and caring for children) into account, women work about 30 minutes more than men every day, which amounts to 39 days per year.

13 98% of people who stay at home to care for family are women.

14 22% of TDs in the Dáil are women.

15 The part of the brain that weighs options before making a decision (the anterior cingulate cortex) is larger in women than men.

16 Women use 13,000 more words per day than the lads do.

17 The tallest ever woman was Zeng Jinlian from China, who, at 8 feet 1¾ inches, was over a foot taller than Shaquille O'Neal.

18 Women live, on average, 2–5 years longer than men, in every country. This also applies to chimps and orang-utans.

19 Women cry somewhere between 30 and 64 times per year compared to 6–17 times for men (repressed much?).

20 Men lie on average six times per day, which is twice as much as women.

All things considered, we're pretty amazing creatures. Let's always remember that.

AM I A FEMINIST?

If you want to have the same opportunities in life as everyone else, you are a feminist. Full stop. If the word 'feminist' plants a picture in your head of an angry woman who hates men, you're wrong.

Here's the thing: for the most part, we have it good. We can do pretty much anything that a man can do, if we so choose. It's not that long since women who worked in government jobs had to, I kid you not, quit their jobs if they wanted to get married.

But if you look a little closer, you will see that we still have a long way to go. Women in Europe earn 84 cents for every euro that men make. Shockingly, there are more CEOs called John in the UK's top 100 companies than there are female CEOs called anything!

But we can't just blame men for this. More girls than boys graduate every year, but we don't apply for enough of the big jobs. We have so much to contend with in our lives, with pressures to fit in, pressures to look a certain way and pressures to be all things to all people. And those pressures are often put on us by ourselves and other girls.

A feminist wants girls to put the same value on themselves as boys do, to believe that they have just as much to say as boys do and to truly feel that how they look will not dictate the opportunities that are available to them. A feminist will do everything in her power to ensure that every girl she raises, educates or employs will have an easier path than she did.

The National Women's Council of Ireland hold an event for young women aged 16–25 called 'Femfest' every year. Check it out at www.nwci.ie.

FiVE WAYS WE CAN LiFT UP AND SUPPORT EACH OTHER

Over the past few years, there has been loads of talk all over the world about what it means to be a woman, what we can and can't do, what we are or are not worth and how we value ourselves and each other. It's been a revolution, and things are starting to change.

We still aren't paid equally, and we don't have enough representation when it comes to making big decisions that affect all our lives. However, we are starting to speak up and work together to create change, which is a really positive thing. We don't all have to agree with each other or see eye to eye, but we do need to make sure that each and every one of us feels heard and valued, and we must defend each other's right to have choices.

1 **BE SELFLESS** – Don't just get hung up on the issues that concern you and your life personally. All our issues are interconnected on some level or other, and if we all worry about everyone having equal opportunities, we all have more power. Think about your sisters, your schoolmates, your future daughters, if you choose to have them. Fight for what we all deserve, not just what you feel you deserve, and know that others are fighting for you too.

2 **LEARN ABOUT THE ISSUES** – Education is power. Know the facts. Look at an argument, try to understand both sides and form your own views. You don't have to agree with everyone, but you do need to be able to defend and explain your own opinions.

3 **SPEAK UP** – Your voice is your biggest tool. Call people out on their behaviour. Don't let people speak over you because you're young or female, or for any other reason. If someone makes a comment that is inappropriate, calmly explain it to them. They'll get it eventually.

4 **BUILD YOURSELF UP** – Confidence doesn't come overnight, but work on it. You are not a second-class citizen, no matter what anyone else says or thinks. You are a unique and beautiful person with as much right to take up space and be heard as anyone else.

5 **BUILD UP OTHER WOMEN AND GIRLS** – For some reason, we girls often see the negative in each other. Let's change that and focus on the positive in every woman around us. Tell them they're special and beautiful, and smart and worthy. We are not in competition with each other. We can all succeed. Let's support each other.

WHY SHOULD I CARE ABOUT POLITICS?

It's hard to see how politics fits into your life when you're young. Here are Daisy's thoughts on the importance of young people getting involved in politics.

When I was younger, I couldn't get my head around politics. I couldn't understand how these random strangers who I couldn't relate to in any way were making decisions that would directly affect my life. And if we did live in a 'free country', as people kept telling me, why did we need rules in the first place?

My parents didn't take much notice either; my dad said they were 'all a shower of wasters' and threw all the election leaflets into the cat's litter tray. Now I'm a little older, and I used my vote for the first time in the referendum to repeal the Eighth Amendment. This referendum saw young people finding a new passion for activism. People of all ages joined the register for the first time ever. For the first time, I asked myself, 'Why should we care about politics? Especially as young people?'

The answer is simple. As long as we care about politics and exercise our right to vote, our lives are in our own hands. To a certain extent, anyway. You could, of course, opt out in the hope that others will vote *in your interests. But where would that get us? If you don't vote and I don't vote and your best friends don't vote, young voices will be drowned out. I always thought that one vote wouldn't make a difference, but what about a hundred votes? Or a thousand votes?*

As young people, we can often feel powerless over our futures, but being informed about politics and holding our politicians to account is within our power, and we should value that.

Before 1918, women were not allowed to vote at all. That was changed by the suffrage movement, led by the fabulous Hanna Sheehy-Skeffington, Emmeline Pankhurst and Constance Markiewicz, who sacrificed so much to demand that the law be changed to include us. It was a massive achievement by these trailblazers, many of whom were imprisoned. Emily Davison famously died when she threw herself in front of the king's horse at the Epsom Derby as an act of protest.

The Representation of the People Act became law in 1918. It initially only granted the vote to women over 30 who were educated and owned land, but it was a start. Generation after generation of Irish women have built on the fights and victories of those who went before us. Now we will value and use those beautiful, hard-won votes.

Let's not take it for granted. As soon as you turn 18, make sure to get yourself registered, get informed, get involved and get voting. As young people, the world and our future is in your hands.

THE ONLINE WORLD

We live in two worlds: the one we see, feel, touch and smell; and the one that exists online, which we enter through our phones, tablets or laptops.

Our relationships with the real and online worlds are important to us, but to live healthy and happy lives it's important to maintain a balance between the two. Your online life should complement your offline life, but never, ever replace it.

Your online persona should reflect who you really are. Nobody is perfect, and every life has its ups and downs. Don't feel under pressure to create an online persona that filters out every perceived imperfection, and don't buy into other people's filtered realities either. Don't compare your behind-the-scenes to someone else's highlight reel!

BE KIND ONLINE

Think for a second about our place in time.

Billions and billions of lives were lived before we were born. Billions and billions of opportunities to build on the hard work of those who came before us.

We learned how to crush herbs to heal illness, how to make drugs to stop deaths from infection, how to transplant organs. We trained pigeons to deliver messages, invented the telegram and can now have face-to-face conversations with loved ones across the globe.

But we haven't yet learned the single most important lesson of all. How to be kind.

People who seem perfect make us uncomfortable. But people who seem imperfect also make us uncomfortable. In this day and age, with the epidemic of anxiety that we experience, we are given countless opportunities to bring a little light into each other's lives. Positivity is just as infectious as negativity.

Forgiving someone for their mistakes doesn't mean that we condone the behaviour. It is recognising that we are all works in progress, and knowing that, one day, we too will need forgiveness.

We build people up for their talent, then we judge their every move, holding them accountable for our feelings about their actions. When they suffer, we click even more furiously. We have a one-strike-and-you're-out attitude, which can drag another human person into depths of stress and despair that we can never understand.

Before you comment online (or in person), ask yourself three questions:

Is it true?
Is it kind?
Is it necessary?

If not, maybe it doesn't need to be shared with the world.

SOCIAL MEDIA

We love social media. It's a great way to chat to friends, seek inspiration and find out what's going on in the world. But it is good to know exactly what we're dealing with, and research has found that depression linked to social media is two times higher in girls than in boys. Two-fifths of girls use social media for over three hours a day, and that seems to be related to our mood and our sleep patterns. Listen, we have no intention of telling you to get rid of your phone. But if you notice some changes in mood, maybe reduce your time for a few days and see how you feel.

+ **TRACK YOUR ONLINE TIME FOR A COUPLE OF DAYS** – You'll be surprised how much time scrolling you actually do. Some tracking apps will give you a free report, but it might not be pretty! If social media is distracting you from more important things like study or sleep, there are also apps like Cold Turkey, which will ban some sites for specific times.

+ **MUTE YOUR NOTIFICATIONS** – How many times do you pick up your phone, dismiss a notification and put it down again? Silence is golden.

+ **LEAVE YOUR PHONE DOWNSTAIRS** – Your brain needs and deserves a break. Give your phone a bedtime and tuck it into in a kitchen drawer. You can even kiss it goodnight if you want to!

+ **DON'T HIT IT FIRST THING** – Don't pick up your phone before you do anything else. Give your brain a break before you start bombarding it with information. Get dressed, have breakfast and brush your teeth, then knock yourself out.

+ KEEP YOUR HANDS BUSY – A lot of phone use is just a form of fidgeting. Do some colouring, sketching, knitting – or squeeze your sister's blackheads!

Remember, it doesn't have to be all or nothing; life is all about **BALANCE**. Just cut down a little, and see if you notice a difference.

WHY CANT WE ALL GET ALONG?

At heart, most people are good and want what's best for everyone. So why is there so much disharmony and arguing in the world? Just ten minutes on Twitter brings us out in a sweat. Why is everyone so angry?

Good question! The truth is that people all see the same world through different lenses. Everyone comes to a conversation from a different place, and everyone wants to protect what they have.

Most of the big issues that we see come from a lack of understanding or empathy for one another. Or they happen when we 'other' people who are different to us. This is very dangerous because it can stop us respecting different cultures, religions, or ethnicities.

'OTHERING' other people causes us to dehumanise them, and

consider them not to be as deserving as others. People act out of either love or fear, and fear often comes across as disrespect, defensiveness or anger.

That's why it's so important for us to go out in to the world with the belief that every single individual shares the same right to protection, safety, representation and support. Those of us who already have it should fiercely protect those who don't. It's called being **SOUND** – let's all give it a try.

MY STORY: SARAH

WHAT DO I WANT TO BE WHEN I GROW UP?

Sarah shares her valuable advice for figuring out what –
or who – you want to be one day.

I've been me for 19 years now. I've never been anyone else. I should know myself inside out at this stage, shouldn't I?

As it turns out, we don't always know ourselves as well as we think we do. I still can't predict what decision I'm going to make or how I'll react to a given situation. I see my reflection every time I look in the mirror; I know every mole on the back of my hand like, well, the back of my hand, but yet I still don't fully understand what I need, what I'm good at and where I want to go.

Some days I want to travel the world with a one-person tent and a spare pair of knickers in my backpack, the next I want to be a high-flying career woman guiding a team of 50 and having my coffee placed in front of me each morning.

I want beautiful things, but not too much stress. I want my phone to be eternally charged, and I want to be constantly zenned out and relaxed. I want to wear power stilettos to work but be able to switch to fluffy socks when I feel like it. I don't know where my life is going to take me or where I want to take my life, or which will happen first.

Now, at 19, I need to start making some decisions. I've started taking a long hard look at myself. What am I good at? What kind of person am I? What do I need to work on? Where do I fit into the 'real world'?

I don't have the answers, and that freaks me out a little if I'm honest. Sometimes I can't even decide what I want to have for lunch. How the hell can I have my whole life figured out? Maybe I have too many options available to me; can someone help me narrow this stuff down?

From when we're little kids, people ask us what we want to be when we grow up. I think that's where we're going wrong. Instead of asking 'what' we want to be, why not ask us 'who' we want to be? That changes everything!

I've started thinking about the type of person I want to be, who I want to surround myself with and what type of energy I want to put into the world. When I figure that out, it'll be easier to pick the career that lets me be my whole self. The answers will come to us in their own time; we just need to keep trying our best and being patient, surrounding ourselves with people who inspire us, and learning something new every single day.

It makes me feel so much better to know that at the age of 23 ...

- Oprah had just been fired as a TV reporter.
- JK Rowling was struggling to pay her bills.
- And Walt Disney had just been declared bankrupt.

It's all going to be okay. It won't always be easy, but it will be worth it if I have faith in myself. Sometimes, we need to take a few steps backwards, or sideways, or even fall off the road entirely to figure it out. The important thing is to always – no matter what – get back up again.

HOW TO GET YOUR FIRST JOB

We all love being independent, the master of our destiny, having the freedom to decide to go to that festival, buy those trainers or treat ourselves to pizza. To do that we need money, moolah, cash dolla. And the only way to do that is to get a job (or invent something amazing or win *Love Island*).

The most difficult thing about getting a job is that everyone wants you to have some experience. But how do you get experience when you've never had a job? Here are a few tips we've learned about talking your way onto that career ladder. The only way is up!

+ **DON'T GET YOUR MAMMY TO GO AROUND THE TOWN ON YOUR BEHALF** – Every time a mammy hands a CV in to an employer, it gets chucked straight in the bin. If you can't be bothered dragging your butt out of bed to find a job, you have a long way to go before you can actually do one. Seriously. Come on. You're better than this.

+ **GET A GOOD CV** – Not all your experience has to be paid. Do you coach a sport, help fundraise for a cause, babysit your little cousin or do the odd Saturday in your auntie's sweet shop? Stick it down. To be clear, do not lie, but don't be afraid to sell yourself. Relatedly, if your email address is sleeping4life@dosser.com, change it to something more professional before you add it to your CV. Oh, and on another related note – use spell check!

+ **IF YOU CAN'T GET A PAID JOB THIS SUMMER, DO SOMETHING TO IMPROVE YOUR CHANCES NEXT YEAR** – Try to find someone who will let you work for free (for a few weeks) in return for training and a good reference. If you can get some barista training in a coffee shop, you're laughing. And if you make a good impression they might even keep you. Alternatively, volunteer at a local charity. You never know, you might even enjoy yourself or learn something.

+ **IF YOU MANAGE TO GET AN INTERVIEW, DON'T PRETEND YOU KNOW IT ALL ALREADY** – You don't, and no one will buy it. Admit that you will need training, but assure the interviewer that you learn quickly and will work hard. Be polite and make you sure you thank them for their time.

Finally, if you don't get a job straight away, keep trying. Most places get lots of applicants over the summer and it's generally a case of being in the right place at the right time. Good luck!

WHY WORK ETHIC IS SO IMPORTANT

Do you ever look at successful women and wonder how they got so lucky?

That's your first mistake. Very few people do well based on luck alone. Most of the women who are at the top of their game have got there through steely determination and a relentless work ethic.

Malcolm Gladwell (an expert on experts) says that it takes 10,000 hours of practice to become an expert at anything. That's a lot of hours, but it's reassuring because it means that anyone can achieve anything if they work at it. Talent and luck will get you so far, but only blood, sweat and tears will get you to the top. That's why it's so important to follow your passion, because you have to really love and believe in what you're doing not to quit on hour 9,998.

'There is no passion to be found in playing small – in settling for a life that is less than you are capable of living.' NELSON MANDELA

'Work B**ch!' BRITNEY SPEARS

A REMINDER THAT THERE'S ALWAYS ANOTHER WAY

I have no idea what I got in my Leaving Cert. That is God's honest truth. From the day I opened that A4 envelope to this day, I have never even looked back at it.

I can tell you that I passed – barely. I was going through all sorts in my life at the time, and I was struggling to keep my head above water. I had no clue what I wanted to do with my life or how to get there. I was in my early twenties before I enrolled in night classes, and I now hold a bachelor's and a master's degree (although I still can't spell). What's for you won't pass you, but it will wait until the time is right.

Some of us are academic, and if you are, great. You will surely excel in college, just as you did in secondary school. Here's some fireworks just for you. Well done! Some of us are smart, creative, entrepreneurial, artistic, insightful, hardworking, adventurous, fearless, capable and imaginative, but not academic. The key is to find your passion, and to use all your resources to find another path to achieving your dreams.

Those who rise to the top are not necessarily those who excel in school. Those who succeed are those who want it the most, who have a good attitude and a solid work ethic. It is those who reflect on and learn from their mistakes and never, ever give up.

SOME FINAL HOME TRUTHS TO LEAVE YOU WITH

Much as our friends and family tell us we are wonderful, perfect humans, the truth is that many of us could do with hearing a few home truths every now and again. When thinking about who you are, the type of person you want to become and how you want people to remember you, there are a couple of pointers that might sting a little, but are the truth – pure and simple.

So brace yourself, this will only hurt a little:

1 **YOU ARE ONLY THE STAR OF YOUR OWN MOVIE** – Much as it feels like the world revolves around you, it doesn't. People have their own crap going on, and to everyone else, their crap is more important and urgent than yours. So when you're having a moment of drama, don't expect everyone else to jump to attention. People will help when they can, and then get back to their own drama. It's how life works.

2 **YOU ARE NOT THE ONLY ONE TO EVER EXPERIENCE PAIN** – Is your heart broken? Yeah, it sucks. How do we know that? Because our hearts have all been broken too. Pain is part of life, and no one is immune. It's how you deal with it that counts.

3 **MONEY WON'T MAKE YOU HAPPY** – Okay, we know everyone says this, but it's the absolute truth. Money might relieve your stress slightly, but your level of happiness is not directly related

to how much money you have. See that sun shining outside? Go lie under a tree, watch the leaves dance in the breeze and feel the warmth of the sun on your face. That level of contentment cannot be bought, my friend.

4 **YOU DO NOT DESERVE A PARTNER WHO WILL TREAT YOU LIKE A PRINCESS** – Waiting for a rich guy or girl to come and buy you handbags? Oh no, honey child. You deserve someone who will treat you like an equal, someone you can build a life with, someone who knows you're not perfect, but loves you for being a work in progress. You will need to take care of and be there for each other. That's what true love is.

5 **EVERY GOOD THING IN LIFE WILL SCARE THE BEJAYSUS OUT OF YOU** – Amazing opportunities will come your way if you work hard. But each change, even the good ones, will require you moving out of your comfort zone. That comfort zone is cushy but boring. You will only achieve your potential if you take risks. If you waste your talent, you only have yourself to blame. Feel the fear and do it anyway.

6 **NOT EVERYONE LIKES YOU** – People are like ice cream flavours. Some love mint choc-chip, and it makes others gag. Mint choc-chip is not good or bad, it's a matter of taste. Stop trying to suit everyone, or you'll end up vanilla. And the world has enough vanilla.

7 **TO SUCCEED, YOU NEED TO *WERK*** – Talent and luck might be your friends, but if you sit waiting for it all to fall into place, you'll end up with haemorrhoids. Work like your life depends on it. Because it does.

8 YOUR PARENTS ARE NOT YOUR MAIDS – The more your parents
   do for you, the less you will be able to cope with real life. Pick up
   your own socks.

9 BE THANKFUL FOR WHAT YOU HAVE – You are lucky. Someone
   loves you. Your life is good. Stop focusing on the negative and BE
   GRATEFUL.

RESOURCES

IF YOU NEED ANY MORE INFORMATION ON ANY OF THE THEMES MENTIONED IN THIS BOOK, THERE ARE LOTS OF BRILLIANT RESOURCES ONLINE. IF YOU'RE STRUGGLING WITH YOUR MENTAL HEALTH, THE FIRST STEP IS USUALLY TO MAKE AN APPOINTMENT WITH YOUR GP, WHO CAN ADVISE YOU BASED ON YOUR INDIVIDUAL NEEDS.

OFTEN THE HARDEST THING IS TO ADMIT YOU NEED SOME HELP AND REACH OUT TO SOMEONE. BUT DO IT, YOU'LL BE GLAD YOU DID. THE MOST AMAZING, COMPASSIONATE, SUCCESSFUL AND INSPIRING PEOPLE I KNOW ARE THOSE WHO FACED CHALLENGES AND MANAGED TO OVERCOME THEM. HANG IN THERE, IT WILL PASS.

AsIAm is Ireland's national Autism charity and advocacy organisation, providing information and advice. (www.asiam.ie)

Ask About Alcohol is a valuable source of information about alcohol and other related matters, such as physical and mental health. (www2.hse.ie/alcohol)

Aware provides support and information to people whose lives are affected by depression, bipolar disorder, postnatal depression or suicidal thoughts. (www.aware.ie)

BeLonG To is the national organisation that supports lesbian, gay, bisexual, transgender, and intersex (LGBTI+) young people in Ireland. (www.belongto.org)

Bodywhys provides online, phone and group support for people affected by eating disorders. (www.bodywhys.ie)

Childline is a private, confidential listening service for young people under 18 in Ireland. It can be contacted for free, by phone or online, 24 hours a day, every day. (www.childline.ie)

Drugs & Alcohol Helpline is a free and confidential helpline for any questions or concerns about drugs or alcohol. (www.hse.ie/go/drugshivhelpline)

Dublin Rape Crisis Centre is a national organisation that offers a wide range of services to any person affected by rape, sexual assault, sexual harassment or childhood sexual abuse. (www.drcc.ie)

Dyslexia Association Ireland offers information and support services for people affected by dyslexia. (www.dyslexia.ie)

Jigsaw offers free mental health support services for young people aged 12–25. (www.jigsaw.ie)

MyContraception.ie provides information and advice on contraception and the different contraceptive options available.

MyOptions.ie provides free and confidential information and support to people experiencing an unplanned pregnancy.

MyMind provides affordable face-to-face or online counselling and psychotherapy. (www.mymind.org)

National Association for Victims of Bullying provides counselling for those who bully and victims of bullying via a telephone support line. (Tel: 057 9331590)

Pavee Point Traveller and Roma Centre advocates for improvement in the quality of life and living circumstances of Travellers and Roma in Ireland. (www.paveepoint.ie)

Pieta provides free, specialised support to people who engage in self-harm, suffer with suicidal ideation, or are bereaved by suicide. (www.pieta.ie)

Plan International Ireland works to advance children's rights and promote equality for girls. (www.plan.ie)

Positive Options provides advice and support for those experiencing unplanned pregnancies. (www.mypositiveoptions.org)

Rainbows Ireland helps children and young people who have experienced bereavement, or a significant loss such as parental separation or divorce. (www.rainbowsireland.ie)

Samaritans provides a confidential helpline, 24 hours a day, for people experiencing feelings of distress or despair, or suffering with suicidal ideation. Call 116 123. (www.samaritans.org)

SexualWellbeing.ie provides information on sexual health, consent, unplanned pregnancy, treatment and prevention of STIs, and more.

ShoutOut provides workshops to schools, parents and teachers to help improve the lives of LGBTQ+ people. (www.shoutout.ie)

SpunOut.ie provides helpful, reliable information on topics relevant to young people, free of any shame or bias, including physical, mental and sexual health.

TackleBullying.ie TackleBullying. ie is a website with lots of resources for children, parents and teachers on dealing with bullying and cyberbullying.

Teenline is a national listening and support service for children and young people up to the age of 18, which is run by the ISPCC. (www.ispcc.ie/teenline)

The **Transgender Equality Network Ireland** (TENI) works to improve the lives and advance the rights of trans people and their families. (www.teni.ie)

Turn2Me offers professional support and counselling for anyone feeling anxious, sad or lonely. (www.turn2me.ie)

Webwise offers free information, advice, education and resources to help parents, teachers and students address internet safety issues. (www.webwise.ie)

Women's Aid provides advice and practical support for women and children who are being physically, emotionally and/or sexually abused in their homes. (www.womensaid.ie)

The National Women's Council of Ireland (NWCI) is the leading national women's membership organisation which seeks to achieve equality between men and women. (www.nwci.ie)

Young Social Innovators (YSI) encourages, motivates and creates new opportunities for young people to actively participate in the world around them and help to build a fairer, more equal society. (www.youngsocialinnovators.ie)

YourMentalHealth.ie is a site that contains lots of helpful information and advice on mental health issues and coping with difficult situations.

National Youth Council of Ireland represents all voluntary youth organisations in Ireland and acts on issues that impact young people. (www.youth.ie)

ACKNOWLEDGEMENTS

—

To Sarah Liddy, Aoibheann Molumby and the entire team at Gill for offering me this opportunity to fulfil my earliest dream, and for making the process almost too easy.

To all the team at Shona: the board, the volunteers, the ambassadors, the supporters and the friends. I started The Shona Project as a tribute to the life I never got to share with my sister. Now I have an army of sisters, which has been the greatest joy of all. I'm so proud of what we've achieved together.

Special thanks to the following team members who contributed their stories to this book, and to many more who have opened their hearts to us over the years: Alana Daly Mulligan, Alexandra Day, Amber Dowling, Steph Golds, Siobhan Murphy, Sophie Kane, Ciara-Beth Ní Ghríofa, Abigail McDonnell, Alannah Owens, Megan Devaney, Rebecca Garvey, Orna Murray, Niamh Clarke and Dr Sharon O'Donnell.

To the Heffernan and Darcy families, who have been hugely encouraging and supportive always.

In fairy tales, the helpless princess sits in the tower waiting for her prince to come and save her. The real fairy tale happens when the prince and princess fall in love, take care of each other, believe in each other and build a beautiful life together. Ferg, when I think of the word 'home', I think of you.

To Sean, Freya and Zach – my greatest teachers – I am so proud of you all. Never forget how precious you are to me, and to each other.

ABOUT THE AUTHOR

—

Tammy Darcy is an award-winning social entrepreneur. She founded the Shona Project to provide a safe place for girls to seek guidance and advice on all the challenges associated with growing up in Ireland. Backed by a team of professional advisors, the website also provides girls with an opportunity to share their own stories and learn from each other. The Shona Project has also delivered workshops to almost 13,000 girls in schools across Ireland.

NOTES